JAKE'S MOUNTAIN ROAD

Other publications by

Wayne Clawson

Short stories: "Bungee Tales" and "Buff is Dead"
included in the High Country Writers 2014 anthology
Headwaters II

Wayne Clawson is a native of Boone, North Carolina. He graduated from Appalachian High School and Appalachian State University. He was voted the most valuable player of his high school football team and selected as a captain for the University football team. After his military service to the United States Air Force, Wayne returned to Boone to join the advancement staff at his alma mater. He retired as Associate Vice Chancellor from the University in 2004. Wayne and his wife Joy have two children (Amber and Whitley) and three grandchildren, Landon, Berrin and Tice.

JAKE'S MOUNTAIN ROAD

The Murder of Jeni Gray, the Kidnapping of Leigh Cooper and the Trial of Daniel Brian Lee

by Wayne Clawson

Best wishes, Dayton

Wayne

Wayne Clawson
384 Dougherty Farm Lane
Boone, NC 28607
828-964-5748

Cover photo by Wayne Clawson
Photos from the estate of Leigh Cooper Wallace
and archives of the *Watauga Democrat*
Book design by Luci Mott

ISBN-13: 978-1987776768

ISBN-10: 1987776763

This book is dedicated to the memory of Jeni Gray and Leigh Cooper Wallace.

The book was made possible through the assistance of a number of extraordinary individuals. Technical expertise and exceptional professional guidance were provided by Judith Geary. Endless patience and encouragement were the gifts of Joy Clawson. Special appreciation for abundant cooperation is due the extraordinary Cooper and Wallace families (Claude and Louise Cooper, and Leigh and Chris Wallace).

On behalf of the citizens impacted by their work, this author wishes to extend admiration for and appreciation to Defense Attorney Chester Whittle, District Attorney Tom Rusher, and the entire law enforcement and justice communities of Watauga County, the Town of Boone, and the State of North Carolina, who worked so diligently and effectively in the interest of justice in this case.

Thanks also to Tom Meyer and the Watauga Democrat for their cooperation regarding photographs and background information for the story.

Proceeds from the sale of this book will be directed to the Jeni Gray scholarship fund at Appalachian State University and the Leigh Cooper Wallace Scholarship Fund at Watauga High School.

JAKE'S MOUNTAIN ROAD

Introduction

It happens each fall at Appalachian State University in the mountains of western North Carolina: The Walk for Awareness. People gather at night near the steps of the Dougherty Administration Building—students, faculty, townspeople. The autumn air is always cool and crisp. The sky is big. A small bell chimes every three minutes; although not loud, the sound is clear and distinct and commands attention.

Influential individuals from the campus and the town make speeches. The importance of something referred to as "awareness" is addressed. The virtues of common sense and caution are extolled. Participants are reminded that a rape occurs every three minutes in this country, every time the bell chimes. The observation is made that not all people have our best interests at heart; some would, and for a multiplicity of reasons, do us harm. When the speeches are concluded, the assembled walk quietly, reverently, and respectfully—many carrying lit candles—through the campus and the town.

The young students who comprise the bulk of the participants for the walk were not yet born when the tragic events of 1989 that serve as the genesis for "the walk" occurred. For their edification, for posterity, and for those members of the community who never knew the facts, they are recorded within the pages that follow.

The story is taken from live interviews with individuals central to the events and from the transcript of the trial of Daniel Lee. The telling is in support of the two major goals of the Walk for Awareness: To promote an ever-vigilant attitude

9

of awareness related to caution and safety, and, in the words of Dr. Sally Atkins, to acknowledge that, "We must hold each other close; and before it is too late, we must create within ourselves and with each other a new and better way of being."

CHAPTER ONE

The Heinous Crime

Excerpt from District Attorney Tom Rusher's final summary for the State of North Carolina, Murder Trial of Daniel Brian Lee, April 25, 1990:

"Ladies and gentlemen of the jury, on the Sunday morning of September 24, 1989, Jeni Gray got up early. Her self-discipline called for her to do so in order that she might take her exercise before meeting her father and attending church. In order to be prudent and safe, she did not go to some remote or isolated spot; she drove right into the middle of the little town of Boone where she parked her car to begin her walk.

"Now, Boone, North Carolina, is Jeni Gray's hometown. It is my hometown. One ought to have the right to stroll the streets of our beautiful, mountain town in safety. However, on that fateful morning, Jeni was denied that right. And, ultimately, she was denied the right to live; for she encountered on those normally peaceful streets, a killer: Mr. Daniel Brian Lee, a man who kills for fun."

Daniel Lee arose early on the morning of September 24, 1989, as well. The horrendous weather of the previous two days had passed. Although the brunt of Hurricane Hugo had fallen on South Carolina and central North Carolina, the mountains to the west were assailed by the residue of the winds, rain, and flooding caused by one of the most powerful storms ever to strike the southeastern United States. Trees were down over the entire region; power outages were widespread. However, that particular Sunday morning dawned bright and clear.

Mr. Lee, a dishwasher and kitchen worker at the Blowing

Rock Hospital, called his employer and reported the condition of the road to his house would not permit him to make it to work—a lie. He just did not care to work that day, for he had other plans. Said plans called for a hunting expedition: he would seek out a female victim to abduct and force to satisfy the sexual desires and fantasies that consumed him.

The final summary for the State of North Carolina continues:

"Now, this man, Daniel Lee, kidnapped Jeni Gray from the streets of her hometown. He took her to a lonely, remote place on Jake's Mountain. We don't know exactly what he did to her there. We can only imagine. And, if you're like me, you hate to even do that. We do know that at some point in time Jeni was forced to disrobe; she stood naked in the glare of her murderer. We know that she was knocked or forced to the ground. As she lay naked on that ground, she was beaten pitilessly on the head with a club. She was struck repeatedly and so hard that her skull was fractured.

"We do know that Mr. Daniel Lee, not being satisfied with this, then kicked her in the throat numerous times, stood on her back, and took her own garment and choked her to death. And then he left her poor body there exposed to the elements."

A ruling by the court prohibited the State from reporting one of the crime's most heinous acts: Jeni Gray's autopsy revealed that her assailant inserted an air gun and fired BB's into the soft tissues of her vagina. The medical examiner, due to the deterioration of the body caused by the lengthy exposure to the elements, was unable to determine if that particular violation occurred prior to or after the victim's death.

Defense counsel maintained, "North Carolina law holds that what makes a crime especially heinous, atrocious, or cruel is that which is done to a victim during life. Since we cannot know when this act occurred, it must be deemed inadmissible." The court agreed on the legal point and added its concern regarding the "inflammatory and prejudicial nature of this particular evidence." The jury never learned of this gruesome aspect of the crime.

The summary for the State of North Carolina continues:

"This man, this Daniel Brian Lee, is a man without mercy who now requests mercy from you, ladies and gentlemen of the jury. He, Mr. Daniel Lee, who had no mercy whatsoever, now asks that you grant him mercy. He, Mr. Daniel Lee, who showed nothing but contempt and disrespect for human life, now begs that you spare his life. And that's what this trial is all about."

And, essentially, that's what this story is all about. The following pages reveal the whole story; it is important to know the whole story in order to appreciate the magnitude of the effort expended to ensure the defendant received justice. Justice and life itself were denied Jeni Gray. Although richly deserving of justice, she got none. Her murderer ultimately admitted his guilt and threw himself upon the mercy of the court.

Initially, the determination of an appropriate punishment seemed an easy task for the jury: What circumstances could possibly mitigate the actions of the defendant or render them even remotely possible to understand? Sometimes, however, circumstances are not as straight-forward as they seem. If the degree of punishment was so apparent, why, at the trial's conclusion, did one juror say, "The trial demanded every second of waking consciousness. It repulsed each good- natured thought. It forbade every pleasant dream." Why did another juror comment, "During the time of testimony and deliberation, life became the trial; normal life was hard to remember." Why did all the jurors agree that events in their lives would henceforth and forevermore be referenced in the context of whether they occurred before or after the trial of Daniel Lee?

CHAPTER TWO
The Search

On September 24, 1989, Jeni Gray's father waited patiently for her outside the First Baptist Church in Boone, blissfully unaware that his daughter had suffered a tragic and violent death. He only knew that Jeni was late, and it was not at all like her to be late—ever. Mr. Gray's apprehensions grew exponentially after a call to his daughter's roommates revealed she left for her exercise walk hours ago and had not returned.

Roommates shared information related to Jeni's customary route for her walk. Her car was found in a parking lot at the west end of town. The vehicle was locked; Jeni's pocketbook rested undisturbed on the front seat. Mr. Gray quickly reported his daughter's disappearance to the Sherriff. His action initiated the largest search effort for an individual ever to transpire in the mountains of North Carolina.

Jeni, a reporter/writer for the Appalachian State University News Bureau, formerly worked the crime beat for the local paper, the *Watauga Democrat*; her previous close working relationship with law enforcement made her disappearance a personal matter for the authorities. When Sherriff "Red" Lyons was informed Jeni was missing, he reacted immediately and contacted his friend and Boone's Chief of Police, Zane Tester. Tester shared the Sheriff's opinion that the circumstances warranted immediate attention.

Officers were dispatched to cover every inch of the path it was believed the victim walked. They searched empty buildings, explored adjacent paths, and questioned residents regarding any unusual activity occurring during the critical time period.

The day after her disappearance, authorities distributed a flyer bearing Jeni's photograph throughout the area. The haunting picture of the sweet face with the huge, dark eyes soon appeared in every business window, at the exit and entrance to every University building, and on the doors of every agency in the county and the town. It accompanied every pizza delivered to Boone residents or university residence halls.

Jeni Gray, as her photo appeared in *Watauga Democrat* - **September 1989**

Boone Police issued an alert which was published on the front page of the local paper, *Watauga Democrat*, and announced on the local radio station, WATA. The agent for United Press International issued a bulletin on the wire; Associated Press quickly followed suit. Local residents volunteered and carried out searches of campgrounds and the shores of nearby lakes.

Chief Tester and Sherriff Lyons jointly contacted the North Carolina State Bureau of Investigation to request assistance. On two consecutive days, police and community volunteers established roadblocks at the primary access points to the town of Boone. All vehicles were halted: "Were you in this vicinity last Sunday? Did you notice anything unusual? Did you then or have you since seen the girl in this picture? Please contact us if you see or hear anything related to this disappearance."

Divers gathered at the duck pond in Tomlinson Park on the University's campus. They garnered a great deal of attention as they prepared for the operation. University students were drawn to the strange sight of high-stepping frogmen approaching the water. The circle of the curious grew as the divers disappeared into the depths. For hours, a morbid drama was played in frustrating repetition: alien-looking heads with single, oval eyes protruded from the water, looked to the shore, slowly turned from side to side, and then submerged into the heart of the concentric circles created by their arrival.

The scope of the search for Jeni Gray was testimony to her value to the community. She was so much more than the brief and cold description released to the news media: "A twenty-seven-year-old female with brown hair, approximately five feet three inches tall, weighing one hundred fifteen pounds." A kind and gentle person, she was loved by all who knew her. According to her friend, Nancy Damron, "Jeni epitomizes all that is good in human beings; she brings warmth to a cold day by just being herself."

The dedicated and comprehensive efforts to find Jeni Gray, in almost a week's time, produced not so much as a single lead. The mystery grew each day and weighed heavily upon the minds of the residents of the small, mountain town of Boone. An open letter published in the September 29,1989, edition of the Watauga Democrat, expressed the frustration of the search. The letter was from the hand of Jeni Gray's roommate, Caroline Walker:

"It's a scary thing when someone disappears. You never think it will happen to someone you know, but Jeni Gray disappeared last Sunday from the streets of Boone. Many people miss her and are trying desperately to find her. Karen Addison and I are Jeni's roommates, and her disappearance has affected our lives dramatically.

"Two of the most important things in Jeni's life are her dogs. They miss her terribly. Since her disappearance, they don't eat and their playfulness is gone. They just lie and wait for her return. Karen and I spend a lot of time with her dogs; they are a special part of Jeni that we hold on to tightly.

"Sunday morning Jeni got up early, something she does every day. She wanted to take her exercise before meeting her father for church and lunch. She never saw her father. She never made it to church. She never made it home. So many people have tried earnestly to find her. Karen and I want to thank all the people who are helping with the search and those who have sent their prayers and best wishes for her. I wonder if she knows how many people love her and care about her. I believe in my heart that, wherever she is, God is with her.

"The unknown is so hard to deal with. We have so many questions: What is Jeni going through right now? What is she feeling? Is she alive? Will she ever return? Will we ever find her?"

CHAPTER THREE
The Abduction

The poignant letter written by Jeni Gray's roommate touched Leigh Cooper, a young student at the University. Leigh was one of the students who watched from the bank above the duck pond as the divers searched for a body. She could not help but wonder how someone—anyone —could just vanish without a trace.

Leigh, the daughter of Louise Cooper and Lt. Col. Claude Cooper of the U.S. Army and the Chief Military Science Officer at Appalachian State University, had benefited significantly from her raising and travels as a military "brat." She was a mature and confident young woman. In addition to being a fine student, she was a superb athlete—a stellar runner for the varsity track team.

On Friday, September 29, five days after Jeni Gray's disappearance, Leigh Cooper sat on the bottom step of the staircase at the front of her apartment building anticipating the start of her daily run. The time was 5:45 p.m. Her elbows rested on her knees; the heels of her hands cradled her chin. The air was cool; a light mist was falling.

She left a note propped on the kitchen table for her boyfriend, Chris, that she would return by 6:30 p.m. The timeframe would allow her to run her short circuit of three miles or even the longer five-mile route if she felt energetic. She arose from the step and started into a slow trot. At the end of the parking lot she veered left, lengthened her stride, and began her run in earnest. Her body quickly adjusted to the elevated activity level; the joy of being young and strong and in condition was with her. It was definitely a day for the longer run.

Leigh Coooper running on the road in 1989,
from the book, *Finding Strong*
by Claude Cooper and Leigh Cooper Wallace

A couple of miles into her run, Leigh sprinted up the hill in front of the county medical center, crossed the Blowing Rock Highway, and started down a lightly-traveled road above and behind a local shopping center. She began to anticipate the warm shower that awaited her at the conclusion of her run, and looked forward to her date with Chris that evening.

As she rounded the last turn of a tree-lined curve, the
only segment of her route not lined with houses or businesses
of any kind, she noticed a rusted, old, foreign car at the side
of the road. The car pulled onto the highway toward her. It
slowed to a snail's pace as it neared. Instead of veering left to
provide a cautionary space, the car actually inclined in her direction and forced her onto the narrow shoulder of the road.

Her first thought was that the driver must be someone she
knew, or maybe it was someone in trouble. The mist collected
on the windshield of the car obscured the view of the inside
of the vehicle. The window on the passenger side lowered
slowly as the car rolled to a halt. Leigh approached cautiously.
When she peered in the window, her heart began to pound
and her skin flushed red. She realized the driver of the car was
not someone she knew—or wished to know. The driver was
a menacing, disheveled-looking individual with a scraggily
beard. He leaned toward the open window, rested his right
hand on the passenger seat, and said sternly, "Get in the car."

"Are you kidding?" Leigh said as she recoiled a step back.

The man's eyes dropped to the pistol nestled in his left
hand and returned to Leigh, "Does this look like I'm kidding? Get in the Goddamned car! Listen, if you try to run, I'll
run this car right over your ass or I'll shoot you. Get in the
car! I just want to talk, that's all."

A thousand thoughts flooded Leigh's mind. She could
run, but where? A steep embankment arose from the side
of the road at her back; she would be completely exposed
to gunfire if she tried to climb it. Across the road loomed a
sheer cliff that dropped thirty feet to the rear of the shopping
center below. The car could easily run her down either way
she might try to run on the road. There was little choice but
to obey the demands of the gunman.

Upon entering the car, Leigh buried her face in her hands
and began to cry. Gravel flew as the car sped away. "Please
don't hurt me," she pleaded. "I'll give you whatever you want,
but don't hurt me."

Her captor smiled broadly as he patted her thigh. "Don't you worry, honey. You just do what you're told, and you'll come out of this just fine. I just want you to ride around with me a little, that's all. I just want someone to talk to. I'm not going to hurt you."

For the next five to ten minutes the gunman devoted his attention to driving very fast. It was obvious he had a destination in mind, and wished to attain it as quickly as possible. The heat and moisture generated by the introduction of Leigh's body into the vehicle caused the windows to fog. The driver cursed as he tried to keep the gun pointed at his captive with his left hand and steer the car and wipe the windshield with his naked right hand. The side windows remained fogged even after the defroster had cleared most of the windshield. The inability to see out added to the feeling of isolation and hopelessness Leigh felt.

In spite of the assurances of her captor, Leigh continued to cry and sob. She made an earnest effort to stop crying, but her mind conjured an image of being violated and shot, and the flood of tears returned. She berated herself inwardly for choosing her longer running route; the shorter one would have avoided the barren area where she was abducted.

After what seemed an eternity to Leigh, but was actually only a few minutes, the driver swerved onto the Blue Ridge Parkway. The Parkway, the scenic highway running along the crest of the western North Carolina Mountains, was lightly traveled and ideally suited to the needs of the kidnapper. He visibly relaxed when he reached the Parkway.

"Let's you and me get acquainted," he said. "What's your name?"

"My name is Leigh Martin." Martin is Leigh's middle name. She could think of no immediate advantage to be gained from lying about her name; however, a certain comfort was gained through any level of deception at that point.

"Now, ain't that funny? My name's Lee, too. Only Lee is my last name. As I think about it, you know what that means?

It means if you and me was to get married, your name would be Leigh Lee. Ain't that sweet?" The kidnapper smiled; Leigh sobbed.

"How old are you?" he asked.

"I'm twenty."

"Well, I would have thought you older than that. You know, I'd been followin' you for some time while you ran. I like watching that pretty blond hair flow in the breeze, and I like the way your ass moves when you run."

"Please take me home. No harm has been done. I won't tell anybody. We can forget that anything has ever happened."

"No! That's not gonna happen! We're just gittin' started."

The car accelerated and swerved onto a gravel road. After approximately a half mile, the vehicle slowed at a fork in the road. The main route obviously branched to the left; an extremely rugged and rutted, downhill path veered to the right. As the car inclined to the right and began to jostle and bounce through the gullies and holes, Leigh glimpsed a small wooden sign, barely visible, in the high grass on the left. The sign was weathered and listed slightly to the right. In faded, black letters it proclaimed: Jake's Mountain Road.

Darkness was falling as the old white Datsun disappeared down the foggy throat of Jake's Mountain. The driver leaned forward and steered with intense concentration as the car bounced through ruts and around large rocks. Presently, a wide place in the road was reached. The car was stopped, the engine extinguished, the parking brake applied.

The departure of the engine whine was replaced by an abrupt and ominous silence. Leigh heard nothing but her pounding heart and the deep breathing of her tormentor. The dreariness of the atmosphere wilted her hope for survival. A low, resonant voice issued from the face silhouetted against the window, "This is the place. Now, take off your clothes."

CHAPTER FOUR
THE VIOLATION

D on't do this. Don't hurt me," Leigh pleaded. "You said you wanted to talk. You said you wouldn't hurt me!"

"Yeah, well, I didn't say I wasn't goin' to fuck you, did I? Now, take off them damned clothes!"

"You won't get away with this," Leigh cried. "Please don't do this!"

"Are you goin' to take them Goddamned clothes off or am I goin' to have to rip'em off you!"

Leigh whimpered as she removed her clothes, an easy task since she was wearing only shoes, a tee shirt, bra, running pants, and panties. Her attacker jerked her panties and bra from her hands as they were removed and shoved them into the glove compartment. He confided, "They'll make a nice little reminder of this, won't they?"

After a brief period of admiring and running his hands over the nude body beside him, the kidnapper launched into a flurry of activity as he attempted to remove all of his clothes at once. He pulled, tugged, untied, unzipped, unbuckled, pushed down, pulled off, and discarded all. When finished, he hit the lever to recline the passenger seat. As he pushed her back, he apologized, "These quarters are a little cramped, but we're just gonna have to make do."

Leigh instinctively placed her elbows and knees together as he climbed on her. "Don't do this!" she shouted.

"Listen here!" he responded as he grasped her wrists and pulled her arms apart. "This ain't goin' to be so bad. It'll be over sooner if you don't fight me. Now, don't fight me. Everything's gonna be fine soon."

She was surprised at the ease with which he separated

23

her arms. The pain he inflicted on her wrists was ample proof that her strength was no match for his. He forced his knee between her legs and settled in to begin the rape in earnest. It lasted approximately an hour. No position or activity was excluded.

Leigh attempted to disengage her mind from the predicament of her body. For the first time, she noticed how badly the car smelled -- a sickly vapor of marijuana smoke, spilled beer, and stale body odor. As her rapist writhed and thrusted and groaned with pleasure, she wondered how long she had been gone and if anyone had started to look for her. Regrettably, she was now aware of how someone could just "vanish without a trace."

She began to think of the gun as a potential ally. Her father always said that guns make fickle friends: their loyalty always to the finger on the trigger, their wrath to the direction of the barrel. The gun was outside of her reach, sheathed in the map pocket of the driver's side door. She determined to conserve her energy and seek an opportunity to obtain it and enlist it to her support. It would not be easy; however, if her attacker dropped his guard, she vowed to herself to acquire the weapon and use it without hesitation.

At times, the exertions of the rapist reached a fever pitch. Occasionally, however, the activity slowed. In order to prolong the ecstasy, it was necessary for him to reduce the delightful friction and postpone the consummate pleasure. Leigh was at that point almost anesthetized to the attack. She hoped his exertions would drain his energy and work somehow to her advantage.

She spied a six-pack of empty beer bottles in the foot-well behind the driver's seat. The long neck of a bottle might serve as a passable handle, she thought; the bottle could inflict considerable damage if landed with enough force to a person's face or head. But would the possible gain be worth the risk? If the strike failed to knock him unconscious, it would surely arouse his anger and precipitate a violent retaliation.

And what if the bottle broke but did not render him unconscious? And what if he then gained possession of the bottle? She abandoned the thought.

At a lull in the activity, the attacker extended his arms and hovered over his victim. He whispered, "I saw you runnin' last week. I couldn't get in a position to get you then, and it wasn't 'til Sunday mornin' I was able to find somebody. "

Leigh's body stiffened. She had tried so hard to reject any notion that her circumstances might be related in any way to the disappearance of Jeni Gray.

"Have you been readin' the papers? Well, I'm the one that got Jeni Gray. I read in the paper that she was a friend of the Sherriff and the Police Chief. You ain't their friend, are you?"

"No," Leigh responded meekly.

"Well, she was and it didn't help her a Goddamned bit 'cause I got her anyway. In fact, she's right down the road. Would you like to see her?"

Leigh asked hopefully, "Is she alive?"

"Well, no, she ain't alive. After I raped her, she ran and I had to catch her. I beat her on the head with a big stick, and you know that girl was still alive. So I just kicked her and wrapped her shirt 'round her neck and stood on her back and choked her to death!"

Tears slowly glided down the side of Leigh's face and fell to make a faint tapping sound on the seat. She was then painfully aware of the full magnitude of her situation. Her tormenter was not only a rapist—he was a murderer as well.

"So, now you know, and you must know by now that you're going to have to die, too, right? You didn't really think I was ever goin' to let you go? You didn't really think that, did you?"

The rapist reached over the driver's seat and retrieved the gun from the map pocket. He put the barrel to his captive's temple, "Jeni Gray died a slow, painful death. I killed her with my bare hands. Do you wanna die a slow death or a fast death?"

Leigh cried uncontrollably and closed her eyes tightly.

He whispered, "Trouble talking? Well then, you just nod once if you want a fast death, or twice if you want a slow death. Goddammit, I said, nod once if you want a fast death or twice if you want a slow one!"

Leigh nodded once. The killer pressed the barrel of the gun to her temple and pulled the trigger. A clicking sound was the result, then another, and still another.

"It's empty, honey; and the truth is, it ain't even a real gun. It's a Goddamned B.B. gun. But it *looks* real, don't it? So, the fact is, I guess you're gonna have to die a slow, painful death anyway. I'm gonna have to kill *you* with my bare hands, too."

The rapist's threats produced an unintended reaction within his victim: she rallied. She realized that she had pitied herself long enough and to no avail. Her survival depended upon her ability to think clearly. She was then in possession of a very important bit of information: her attacker was a killer. It wasn't much, but it was more than poor Jeni Gray had up to the moment of her death. Leigh put a halt to the crying and committed herself to endure.

The rapist continued his exertions. Finally, he stopped and was taken by the telltale, quaking motion of orgasm. He sighed and fell limp on top of his victim. Her arms were lax at her sides.

Finally, he said softly, almost sweetly, "Now, hold me and tell me that you love me."

She wrapped her arms around him and whispered numbly to the ceiling, "I love you."

"Say it agin."

"I love you."

CHAPTER FIVE
The Cultivation

At long last, the rapist pushed off his victim and collapsed over on his back to the driver's seat. He leaned up and pulled a marijuana joint and a lighter from the glove compartment. Lighting up, he flopped back to the driver's seat in exhaustion—drawing deeply, exhaling mightily. The glow at the end of the joint punctured the darkness. The rape, for the time being at least, was at an end.

Leigh arose from the seat. She fumbled with the cigarette lighter on the dash and flicked the flame on. "It's so cold and dark in here," she said.

The rapist sat up and started the car. He turned on the heater, and offered her a hit from his joint.

"I'm a runner," she said. "I've never touched any of that stuff."

"Well, Goddamn! I just told you I was gonna have to kill you. You ain't gonna die from smokin' between now and then. Aw, c'mon, try it; you'll like it. Don't it smell nice? I said try it!"

Leigh drew on the joint. She choked and gagged.

He smiled, "Well, I guess you got to get used to it. But, I'll tell you this, after you smoke some of that stuff, you'll get horny and hungry. Yes sir, it'll make you want to fuck and then eat—or eat and then fuck. It don't matter which is first. Here, take another hit. You'll get used to it. You'll like it."

The light from the car's radio coupled with the minimal warmth generated by the car's heater lifted Leigh's spirits slightly. The interior of the old Datsun was flooded with light when the attacker finally threw open the door on the driver's side. He placed his shoes on the ground, and stood on them as he dressed himself. Leigh turned on her side facing him; her arms clung to her knees, which were drawn up under her chin.

"Git outta the car," he said as he slipped on his shoes.

She exited on her side of the car and stood by the open door. Her torso was divided on a diagonal by the light, the lower two thirds of her body was bathed in a dim yellowish hue; her upper body was in the shadows. She instinctively shielded her crotch with her hands. Her weight shifted from one bare foot to the other to escape the cool, wet leaves.

Leigh peered both up and down the Jake's Mountain Road and considered running. If she bolted up the road, he would have the angle and could easily cut her off; however, if she were to sprint down the road, a bit of lead might be gained—he would have to come all the way around the car. The combination of a lead and her running ability might allow her to out-distance him. But she was barefoot and naked; and she knew Jeni Gray had selected that option—with disastrous results.

"Can I put my clothes back on?

"Well, no, we're gettin' rid of them." He leaned into the car, grasped her clothes, and carried them to the other side of the road where he threw them over a steep embankment. Returning to the car, he pulled a pair of jeans and a t-shirt from the trunk and told her to put them on. When she returned to the passenger seat, she passed the tense moments using her finger to rewind a cassette tape she found between the front seats of the car.

In time, he finished his joint and returned to the driver's seat where he sat with his hands clasped together between his legs, his shoulders curled inward against the chill of the night.

"I strung it out pretty good this time. I came a lot quicker with Jeni than with you. Guess I'm gittin' more experienced."

A heavy silence prevailed. Leigh intruded on the quiet, "It sure is a dark, cold night, isn't it?"

"It sure enough is. Do you reckon they're lookin' for you yet?"

"Oh, no. Why nobody will even know I'm gone until Monday when I'm supposed to meet my first class. I talked with my parents on the phone before I left to run. They're back in Kansas. (Leigh's parents were in Boone. Her father's last duty station was in Kansas.) They think I will be studying in the library nearly all weekend. Nobody will miss me."

"You know, it might be a shame to kill you now if nobody is even goin' to miss you 'til Monday. "

"That's right. You know, you told me all this wouldn't be so bad, and you were right. I enjoyed it a lot— except the part about us being all cramped up in this car. I wish we could have done it at my apartment. Hey, why don't we go there and get into my bed?"

"No, Goddammit! We'll do it right here!"

The suggestion was clearly too much too soon. She held up the re-wound tape and asked what was on it.

"Heavy metal. That's what I like, heavy metal." He shoved the tape in the player and cranked up the volume. A dragging, distorted sound gradually became recognizable as that of a heavy metal band. The rapist's head began to nod in rhythm to the music—slightly at first but then awkwardly and in an exaggerated manner. He bumped up the volume to an ear-splitting level, and began to sway from side to side, his long hair brushing his shoulders. The music, of course, called for another joint. Soon the car was fogged with smoke. He shouted, "What kind of music do you like?"

Leigh turned down the volume of the tape slightly and said loudly, "I guess I like all types of music. This shirt you gave me has 'The Who' on it. Do you like them?"

"Yeah, they used to be my favorites. That shirt is special to me for a couple of reasons. I got it when me and some buddies went to their live concert. It was great."

She reduced the volume of the tape again and said in a normal voice, "You said there were a couple of reasons?"

"Oh, yeah, and it was the shirt I was wearing when I killed Jeni Gray."

Leigh was not prepared for the revelation. A sickly, help- less smile froze on her face as she realized she was trapped in a bizarre dream where nightmarish music blared and rape and murder were referred to in the most casual manner. Her skin fairly crawled at the thought of the shirt being next to her.

Finally, mercifully, the music ended and quiet returned. The cultivation continued, "You said, your last name is Lee. So, what's your first name?"

"Daniel."

"Oh, a nice biblical name—Daniel."

"Yeah, I guess. I reckon I wouldn't know much about that."

"You know, Daniel, you were right about that joint: it sure has made me hungry. I just remembered, I haven't eaten anything since breakfast. Let's go get something to eat."

"Well, you know, I've got a pizza in the freezer at home. I could fix that for you. In fact, I'd kind of like to take you home, especially since I ain't got to kill you 'til Monday. It's a good situation for both of us, right? You get to live 'til Mon- day, and I get to fuck you all weekend."

Leigh saw him smile in the dim light from the radio. "Yes, well, I guess you're right there. But you know what? I'm still hungry. Can we stop and get something to eat?"

"I don't have enough money to take you some place, but I got to stop and get gas. I'll get you a little somethin' then. And I'll fix you that pizza when we get to my house. I live with my dad. He won't think nothin' of me bringin' you in; I'll just tell him you're my girlfriend. I live upstairs in the back; he don't ever bother me. Let's see," he said, retrieving his wal- let from the dash, "I hope I got enough money to get some gas and you a little somethin' to eat."

A photograph fell from the wallet as he went through it. Leigh picked it up and asked, "Who's this?"

"That's my friend, Booger."

"You know, I don't think I've ever known anyone called 'Booger.' How did he get that name?"

"You don't want to know."

"Is he a nice guy?"

"Yeah, he's full of crap, but I like to hang out with him. We were at a party one time when I passed out, and he took care of me. He thought I had too much to drink, but I didn't. I passed out from my aneurysm. See I had an aneurysm about a year ago. They had to cut my damn head open to fix it. Ever since then I don't have any energy. I've got to take this medicine that keeps me from sleepin', and I'm just worn-out all the damn time. Well, looka here, a ten-dollar bill! I knew that little sucker was in there somewhere. Our problems is solved. I'm gonna get some gas and take you home for the weekend."

"Great," Leigh said as she hugged his arm.

At Daniel Lee's urging, the old Datsun groaned to a start and began to gradually disgorge itself from the Jake's Mountain wilderness. The car quickly returned to a paved surface. A thrill raced through Leigh's body as they began to meet other vehicles on the road. Soon, the car veered into the lot at the 421 Grocery. She watched as her captor entered the store and gave the clerk his ten-dollar bill. He returned quickly and pumped five-dollars-worth of gas.

He opened the driver's door and leaned in, "They've got them big, cream-filled oatmeal cookies on the counter in there. Would you like one of those?"

"Oh, yes. And could I have a grape Nehi? I love those."

"Sure. I'll git you one. Now, you ain't goin' to try anything funny are you? You'll stay here, right? You'll be here when I get back?"

Leigh smiled sweetly, "Of course I will."

"Good. You know what? You're pretty cool. You really are." He closed the door and entered the store. The drinks were in the cooler at the far end of the store. He collected the grape Nehi and the oatmeal cookie. The clerk rang him up but realized he was out of quarters and had to open a new roll. He apologized, opened a new roll, and returned the small change to the hand of his customer.

When Daniel Lee exited the store, he realized immediately his captive was not visible in the car. He rushed forward and peered inside. The car was empty. The parking lot was barren—no people, no vehicles, nothing. He rushed to one side of the store and then, in a dead run, encircled the entire building. Nothing. No one. She had vanished. The kidnapper, rapist and murderer, stood alone and transfixed under the spotlight of the gas pumps at the 421 Grocery, breathing heavily and holding tightly to a grape Nehi and a large oatmeal cookie.

From the summary for the State of North Carolina:

"How cruel? How mean? How depraved? Has this man, Daniel Lee, no mercy? Has he no pity? Has he no conscience? A mere five days subsequent to the murder of Jeni Gray, he abducts Leigh Cooper—again from the streets of our town. And you heard how this violent course of conduct continued. Fortunately, Miss Cooper escaped. She was not released. She managed by the grace of God and her own ingenuity, to escape. Can you think of anything more especially heinous, especially cruel, especially shameless, especially ... especially ... why words fail me! I run out of words to describe the behavior of this man—except to say, once again, ladies and gentlemen of the jury, that this is a man without mercy who now requests mercy of you."

CHAPTER SIX
The Vanishing

Crystal Adams was in the midst of preparing dinner for her husband Jay and dinner guests, Richard and Jamie Watson, when she realized she had no butter. She asked Richard if he would mind driving to the 421 Grocery to get some butter.

"I'll be back before you can get dinner on the table," Richard said as he departed.

It was almost 8:30 p.m. when Richard Watson started his Chevy Blazer and began his quest for butter. He journeyed down the road and pulled into the parking lot of the 421 Grocery; a foreign car was at the gas pumps. As he exited his car, he was startled when a young woman bailed out of the foreign car, breezed by him, and dived across the driver's seat of his Blazer to curl up in the passenger-side floorboard. She was obviously distraught. She said something very excitedly, but the words ran together and were impossible to understand.

Richard stood bewildered at the door. "Young lady what in the world are you doing?"

She looked at him with tears in her eyes and said slowly and distinctly, "I have just been kidnapped and raped by the man who killed Jeni Gray. He's in the store. You've got to help me. Get me out of here. God, please get me out of here!"

Well, thought Richard, *that seems plain enough.* He returned to the driver's seat and started the vehicle. Slowly and deliberately, he selected "reverse" with the shift lever, backed around, returned the lever to the "drive" position, pressed the accelerator, as if a raw egg rested beneath it, and nonchalantly steered the vehicle out of the parking lot and onto the highway. The duration of his stay at the 421 Grocery was less than three minutes.

"I'm taking you to a friend's house," Richard said calmly. "We'll call the police from there. You just stay down." As the Blazer approached the Adams' driveway, Richard checked his rearview mirror to ensure that no one was following. Seeing nothing, he slammed the pedal to the floor, swerved into the driveway, and sped up to the Adams' house. Leigh ejected from the passenger seat before the vehicle came to a complete stop; she was in the house before Richard could turn off the engine and apply the brake.

"He raped me! He raped me! He's going to kill me! Please help me!" Leigh screamed as she burst in the door of the Adams' house. Crystal, Jay, and Jamie sat horrified. Richard entered the door with a befuddled look on his face.

Crystal said, "Richard couldn't have raped you, dear. He just left to get some butter a few minutes ago. And he wouldn't kill anybody!"

"Oh, not him—Daniel Lee! Daniel Lee raped me, and he murdered Jeni Gray! He would have murdered me, too, but I got away!"

Jay reached for the phone to call the police as Crystal and Jamie led Leigh into the bedroom to sit on the bed. Leigh cried on Crystal's shoulder, "He made me wear these clothes. He wore this shirt when he killed Jeni Gray. Do you have something else I can put on?"

"I sure do. Let me find you something."

Leigh asked, "I want to take a shower. Can I do that?"

Crystal cautioned, "Better not, honey. You know they're going to want to take samples and perform tests and such."

"Can I call my parents?"

"Absolutely, the phone's right over there on the bedside table."

When her father answered the phone, Leigh attempted to speak, but the sound of his voice was more than she could bear. Her earnest attempts drowned in a flood of tears. Crystal gently lifted the phone from her hand and spoke with Mr. Cooper. She directed him to her house and conveyed Leigh's request that he notify Chris.

Leigh's parents and her boyfriend, Chris, hurried to her location. There was no difficulty in finding the house as they neared: whirling blue lights, and a circus atmosphere advertised the location for half a mile.

The expected, tearful reunion of the Cooper family ensued. Leigh's mother cried as she hugged Leigh, "We've been looking for you, honey! We've been looking for you! I was sitting at the kitchen table reading the paper, and I came across that letter written by Jeni Gray's roommate. All of a sudden, I felt something was wrong; I felt so alone. And then Chris called and said he was worried about you. We've been looking for you ever since!"

After the brief but glorious reunion, Leigh's family waited in the living room while police conducted a preliminary interview. The officers wished to obtain enough information to allow them to begin the hunt for the kidnapper. When the questioning was through, Leigh was placed on a stretcher and rushed to the hospital.

Gynecologist, Bruce Jackson, responded to the urgent call for assistance from the Watauga Medical Center. He arrived at the hospital at the same time as the ambulance carrying the victim. A nurse handed the Doctor a box as he entered the examining room. The purpose of the box was cast in large black letters on the top: SEXUAL ASSAULT EVIDENCE COLLECTION KIT.

The box contained what Dr. Jackson and his classmates at the University of North Carolina Medical School called an "idiot kit": the instructions were so simple and detailed that, presumably, an idiot could conduct the exam. The program was a sixteen-step plan that ranged from Step One: Break Seal and Open Box, to Step Sixteen: Checklist for Completion of Steps One through Fifteen. The steps between called for the collection of detailed information and every type of specimen and swab imaginable.

Step Fifteen was an information form to be shared with the victim. It provided the locations and telephone numbers for all the rape counseling centers in North Carolina. Dr. Jackson signed the checklist that was step sixteen and said, "Miss Cooper, I have just completed my second rape examination, which is two more than I ever wanted to complete. I am pleased to report that you seem to be in excellent condition physically. That makes me happy. I'm going to report this news to your family, and I'm sure they will be overjoyed. You have my best wishes."

Subsequent to the examination at the hospital, Leigh was escorted to the police station: "This is Special Agent D.S. Wilson with the North Carolina State Bureau of Investigation," began the recorded statement at the Boone Police Station. "The time is 12:52 a.m., on Saturday, September 30, 1989. We are at the Boone Police Department, Investigative Division. Present are myself, Lieutenant Willie Watson, and Sergeant William Greene of the Boone Police, Mr. Claude Cooper, Jr. and his wife, Louise Cooper, and the victim in this case, Leigh Martin Cooper."

For the next hour, Leigh relayed everything she could remember about her terrifying ordeal. The officers were pleased to discover that she consciously and intentionally made mental notes of the occurrences during the period of her captivity. Her recall was nothing short of phenomenal. The veteran lawmen listened in stunned silence as the story unfolded. During the darkest moments, when the victim was threatened with slow and painful death and forced to declare her love to her attacker, the thoughts of the officers strayed to the females in their own lives—their mothers, wives, and daughters. They could not help but wonder: Were they safe? Where was Daniel Lee?

The answer to the question was comforting, for at that approximate moment, Mr. Daniel Lee was standing in the open doorway of his father's house in Triplett, North Carolina. He appeared anything but menacing in his boxer shorts and stocking feet. His hand shielded his eyes from the high beams of three State Patrol cruisers parked at the front of the house.

Sheriff's Deputy, Robert Collins, stood in front of the center car. Just behind, silhouetted in the light, were the ominous forms of three North Carolina State Highway Patrol Officers. Their broad shoulders, draped with ponchos,

Daniel Brian Lee
mug shot

loomed in the heavy mist; their eyes hid in the shadows of broad-brimmed "smokey" hats. Menacing, pump-action shotguns were trained on the figure in the doorway.

Deputy Collins shouted, "Are you Daniel Lee?"

"Yes sir," came the meek reply.

"Well, you better get some pants on, Mr. Lee. The district attorney has some questions he'd like to ask you."

CHAPTER SEVEN

The Second Search

At 11:22 a.m. on the morning following the abduction and rape of Leigh Cooper, a police vehicle entered the driveway of the Cooper home. A police officer and a very serious looking man in a brown suit approached the door of the house. As soon as he was invited in, District Attorney Tom Rusher (pronounced Roo-shur) introduced himself to the victim and her family. He explained the reason for his visit: "Miss Cooper, as you may know, we have the man who attacked you in jail. We also have a considerable amount of evidence which will aid in obtaining a conviction for his crimes. However, a crucial element in seeing that justice is done in this case will hinge upon your willingness to testify. Now I know it will not be easy, but …"

Leigh interrupted, "If you're asking me if I will testify, the answer is yes! Yes, I will. I don't want him to get away with what he's done. I don't want him to ever have the opportunity to do it again."

A huge smile spread across the district attorney's face; it was accompanied by a sigh of relief. He extended his hand to Leigh and, in turn, to her parents. "That's music to my ears, my dear. Soon, I think, we'll be able to break the grip of fear that has held our community. There is much for us to discuss, but right now is probably not the proper time. You have been through a great deal. I know you need your rest. I would like, however, to take the time to compliment you upon the presence of mind you displayed during this ordeal, and to express my admiration for the magnificent manner in which you acquitted yourself."

Leigh smiled shyly, "I suppose I should have run when he first pulled up and pointed the gun at me."

Rusher's brow furrowed as he responded, "Miss Cooper, I thought about that very thing as I rode over here this morning. In many instances the conventional wisdom might be that one would be better off to run. Without doubt, there will be those who contend that you should have run; however, those individuals would be the first to proclaim, if you had run and been shot down or run-over, that you should have gotten in the car. And let me add one more observation: if you had escaped at that point, the next victim might not have, or the next. And we would have no clue as to what happened to Jeni Gray. The game of 'what if' is a useless one. I counsel you against it. Rather, you should devote yourself to the wide range of joyful potential that life now offers you.

"Oh, and by the way, we now have the gun he used to abduct you. And it was a BB gun—just as you said. But don't feel badly about that. It was made to look exactly like a real gun. The exit hole was even recessed into the barrel, so even those with a knowledge of weapons would have thought it a real gun."

"Mr. Rusher, have you found Jeni Gray yet?"

"No, we haven't. And we must not dismiss the possibility that she might still be found alive, and somewhere other than Jake's Mountain. It could very well be that Daniel Lee told you what he did to frighten you. It would not be unheard of at all that he was boasting of something he only imagined."

Leigh's eyes widened at Rusher's last remark. Her gaze darted to her parents but quickly returned to the district Attorney's face, "There are a lot of things I don't know, Mr. Rusher. But there are a few things I know for sure: Jeni Gray is dead. Daniel Lee killed her. She's out there near that Jake's Mountain Road. Now, you may never find her, but I know she's there."

"We'll do our best, Miss Cooper. I promise you that."

And, in truth, the best efforts had already begun. At

first light on Jake's Mountain Road over twenty police officers spilled out of official vehicles. To a man, they were con-
vinced that Jeni Gray was somewhere in close proximity to
the scene of the previous night's atrocities. In the drizzling,
early-morning rain, the officers donned their slickers and
tucked their pant legs into high-topped boots in preparation
for the search.

The term "road" was a compliment to the old logging
path and buffalo trail that challenged the ambition of even
the four-wheel-drive vehicle. The path wound from the rolling hills at the foot of the Blue Ridge Mountains in Wilkes
County to the heights in Watauga County. The terrain was
extremely steep and rocky. The mountain formed a part of
what was known to early settlers as the "Great Appalachian
Barrier." Small streams crossed the road in at least three different places. In the deep gorge that divided the two largest
sections of wilderness, the constant whisper of cool, clear,
mountain water could be heard as it tumbled and bounced
over rocks smoothed by eons of wear.

At first, it seemed the search will be a rather easy matter:
the areas on both sides of the road were divided into grids on
the searchers' maps. The small squares of territory appeared
innocent and non-threatening. Participants were assigned to
cover specific quadrants. The reality of the matter turned out
to be quite different. The extreme inclines often required officers to reach from branch to branch as they traversed the
mountainside. Occasionally they had to drop to hands and
knees and crawl through thick beds of mountain laurel. Bri-
ars shredded raingear and tore flesh as the search extended
beyond the farthest point anyone believed Jeni Gray would
be found.

At one point, a searcher stopped to rest on a boulder in
the incredibly thick underbrush just off the shoulder of the
road. As he attempted to catch his breath, he realized he was
not sitting on a boulder at all—it was an old refrigerator. "Jesus," he said, "if we can't even see a refrigerator in this stuff,

how will we ever find little Jeni?"

At approximately, 4 p.m. the rain began to fall in sheets. The quest was suspended for the day. The exhausted and battered searchers gathered at the coffee pot at the police station. Jake's Mountain had retained its hold on Jeni Gray, and instilled a heightened respect for the wild into her would-be rescuers.

On Sunday morning, October 1, a brigade of authorities descended upon the little home of Jacob Lee in Triplett, North Carolina. Officers carried a search warrant authorizing them to search the premises of the house. Mr. Lee ushered the group to the narrow staircase leading up to his son's room.

During the short climb of the stairs, the officers got their first hint of what was to come. The aroma from the room above thickened with each ascendant step; it became a putrid gravy of foul odors at the head of the stairs, an acrid mixture of marijuana spiced with body odor, cigarette butts and spoiling and molded bits of decaying pizza.

Sherriff Lyons was the first into the room. Suddenly he became animated and began swatting violently with his hands at an invisible enemy in the air: "Gnats! Look out boys! The place is full of gnats!" Lyons braved the storm, and managed to open a window. Over the next several minutes the plague of pesky sentinels was driven out. The search then began in earnest.

The men sifted through the piles of dirty clothes, overflowing ashtrays, record albums and covers, cans of insect spray, and pornographic tapes and magazines. A pair of athletic shoes appeared to have blood stains on the toe and the heel. From the chest of drawers, third drawer down, back right-side, a pair of lady's panties—black Jockey brand, size five—and one Maidenform Bra, were retrieved.

A strange object was drawn from beneath the bed. It appeared to be a folded piece of plastic. When spread on the floor, it was clear the object was some sort of plastic, blow-up doll in the shape and with the likeness of a naked woman. Cavities were clearly visible at the mouth and crotch. The men gazed at the object in silence. No one wished to be the first to acknowledge he knew what it was. Finally, one officer commented, "How in this world could anyone make love to something like that?"

Another officer responded, "Yeah, she sure is ugly."

The joke earned a punch in the arm and a stern look from the Sherriff. But the comment had the intended effect of relieving the considerable tension that had descended upon the room. It allowed the enjoyment of a brief smile in the midst of the serious business of collecting evidence.

On Monday, the search and the rain continued without results. Throughout Tuesday and Wednesday, various squads of law enforcement personnel combed the wilderness and battled the elements. By Wednesday afternoon a swath one-hundred-and-fifty yards wide extending the entire length of the Jake's Mountain Road had been thoroughly searched. By then, some searchers were being directed to other locations, miles distant, where Daniel Lee was known to frequent.

The growing fear in the minds of many was that the killer may have returned to the scene of the crime and buried the body. But there also existed the fading hope that Daniel Lee never killed anyone and was, as Mr. Rusher said, just trying to intimidate Leigh Cooper.

Local attorney, Chester Whittle, was assigned to represent Daniel Lee regarding the rape and kidnapping charges. When the search dragged on and apprehensions rose in the community regarding the fate of Jeni Gray, Mr. Whittle paid a visit to his now infamous client. Daniel Lee was escorted into the small interview room at the jail. The discussion that ensued was extraordinarily one sided. Whittle did the talking. In fact, Daniel Lee uttered only one word.

"You have told me," Whittle began, "that you had no involvement with the disappearance of Jeni Gray. I support your assertions. The law says that everybody has a right to have someone on his or her side and in your case, that's me.

"But right now, let's just suppose. Let's, just for the sake of argument, let's suppose you know where Jeni Gray is. Now, if you know where she is, and if she's on that mountain, they're going to find her. You see, I know Chief Tester and Sheriff Lyons. They're pretty stubborn fellows. If they think she's there, and I happen to know they do, they're going to find her. I mean, if they have to dig up every tree on that damn mountain, they're going to find her. If they find her there, it will confirm everything Leigh Cooper has told them. If that happens, I think you're going to be facing the death penalty.

"Now, on the other hand, if you know where she is and you share that information, it might be worth some consideration on the part of the District Attorney. I don't know what, maybe nothing. But with the death penalty looming, I think you would agree that any consideration is better than none.

"And one more thing, Daniel, if you did take her and if you left her out on that mountain, it's nothing more than the right thing to do to tell somebody where she is. It's the Christian thing to do. I think her family has given up on seeing her alive, but they want her to have a proper burial. You can understand that, can't you? If it were your sister or mother, you'd want that, wouldn't you? Daniel, do you know where Jeni Gray is?"

"No."

CHAPTER EIGHT
The Sadness

On October 9, 1989, Police Chief, Zane Tester, called Lieutenant Donnie Farmer into his office: "Donnie, she's out there somewhere just off that Jake's Mountain Road. I know she is."

"I think she is, too, Chief. But it's been ten days since Daniel Lee was arrested. And we've searched that mountain mighty hard. What if he buried her?"

"Well, even if he buried her, there'll be some sign. I've decided to start the search over from scratch tomorrow. We'll begin once more where Leigh Cooper was raped, and search the whole area again. But this afternoon, I want you and Curtis to get your rappelling gear together and search those cliffs that border the waterfall out there. He might have thrown her off the top. She could be on one of those ledges where we can't see her."

"Can do, Chief. We'll get right on it."

Soon, Lieutenant Farmer and Officer Curtis Main were hiking with rappelling gear down a trail toward the cliffs. It was a crisp, fall day; random splashes of autumn colors appeared in the trees. Farmer noticed and took a small path that branched off to the right; Curtis continued down a lower, wider route.

The Lieutenant approached a large, fallen tree, and was studying how to get around it when an eerie feeling embraced him—a sudden stillness. His head turned from side to side as his eyes combed the area for the source of his apprehensions. Finally, his gaze fell upon familiar but misplaced objects nestled in the leaves to the left of the path: bare feet.

They connected to legs that led to a pale torso and, ultimately, a pallid face punctuated with dark, hollow eyes that stared blankly into infinity. Although the elements and the activity of the forest creatures had taken their toll, Donnie realized immediately he had found the body of his friend, Jeni Gray. He drew his service weapon and fired two shots into the air, the signal for Curtis and other searchers to come.

The crime scene was secured in short order. The securing was a simple matter in this case: cars manned by patrol officers at the top and bottom of the Jake's Mountain road were all that was necessary. The rugged terrain that had shielded the body from the searchers would serve to deter the curious.

Special Agent John Stubbs of the North Carolina State Bureau of Investigation, a crime scene specialist, arrived soon and carried out his duties with a flourish. Before any significant activity was permitted in the area, Stubbs recorded, via his camera, the exact appearance of the scene. He photographed the path leading to the body, the body—from every conceivable angle—various parts of the body, and any and all suspicious or pertinent items or areas of interest within a radius of approximately two hundred feet.

Agent Stubbs took meticulous measurements and recorded exact distances for everything: Jeni's body was just off an old logging path two tenths of a mile from the main road. The path was eight tenths of a mile from the beginning of the road. The incline of the path was determined to be sixty degrees. One item, near the body, drew immediate attention—a rather sturdy stick or limb. It was three feet two inches long, and it was five feet four inches from the body. A very dark, dried material was clearly visible at one end of the club.

When Agent Stubbs' recording of the scene was complete, the area became the center of a great deal of activity. A cadre of professionals roamed seemingly at random over the crime scene; however, their activities were anything but random. Some carried metal detectors in a search for Jeni's keys or other evidence. Others performed their duties as dictated by their training, expertise, or area of responsibility. A casual observer might have surmised these were cold individuals who performed these tasks. They went about their business in close proximity to but with little notice of the nude body of the young woman who was the focal point of their labors. In fact, it was because of their dedication and concern that their concentration was so focused. They were well aware that the best thing they could do for Jeni Gray at that point was to be proficient in their work. In that, they might insure that her murderer never murdered again.

The county medical examiner, Dr. Evan Ashby, conducted a preliminary examination of the body. With great patience and thoroughness, he insisted that proper procedures were followed so that evidence instrumental in determining the exact cause of death or helpful in identifying the murderer would be preserved. The hands of the deceased were inserted into paper bags, which were tied at the wrists. Ultimately, Jeni was carefully lifted, leaves and all, and gently placed in a body bag. The bag was then carried, with care and due respect for its contents, up the path and away from the Jake's Mountain wilderness.

As the news of the discovery found its way into the law enforcement bloodstream of communications, it gathered steam and coursed throughout the arteries of the public media to the general populace. A silent but pervasive and anguished groan arose from the collective breast of the community. It could not be true. But it was true.

Jeni's father, Bob Gray, trembled with rage when he learned of the discovery, rage at the loss he had suffered, rage at the thought that such a crime could happen in a civilized society, rage at his inability to protect his own from such tragic circumstances. To a lesser but still significant degree, a great many others suffered from an inability to understand. They wanted comforting.

On the campus of Appalachian State University, a memorial service was held on October 11, 1989. A huge crowd gathered. The ceremony was covered by five television stations and a multitude representing the print and radio media. The service was initiated via the remarks of no less than the University's beloved Chancellor, Dr. John Thomas.

Dr. Sally Atkins, the President of the University's Faculty Senate was called upon to give expression to the thoughts and feelings of Jeni's friends and co-workers. Slight in physical stature, Sally was barely visible behind the large podium that dominated the stage in the auditorium. Her words came straight from her heart and resonated with all those who knew and loved Jeni Gray:

"Each month on the second Monday, at 3:10 p.m., she sat, with her notepad and pen, over at the left side of the Faculty Senate Meeting Room. All through our long rituals of academic rhetoric, she stayed patiently with us, listening attentively. She worked with us and I came to know and respect and love this beautiful young woman—Jeni Gray.

"I knew that as a newswoman she would be, not only fair and honest, but also kind and gentle. I knew she would sift through our long hours of debate with sensitivity and intelligence and a depth of understanding rare for one so young. Last Monday I tried not to feel how much I missed her. I failed.

"This morning I spoke with a number of Jeni's friends and colleagues. They spoke about her life. They remembered her gentleness, the unassuming way she had of being with people that made them comfortable. They spoke of her love for animals and her generous spirit. They spoke of her playfulness and ready laugh. They spoke of her inner strength and depth. Jeni was a collector of stories. Her stories connected her forever with those she interviewed. She was a weaver of people and her threads connected all of us with her. This is a hard day. We have lost Jeni Gray, and we have lost our innocence.

"We live in a world where violence is so commonplace we cease to feel. Numbly, we watch the daily news or shows, which make violence seem exciting. We try to hold on to whatever sanity, whatever humanity we have left. But the loss of this one special life, this unacceptable death, stops us cold. In this moment, we must rage and cry and grieve and hold each other close. And, before it is too late, we must begin to create within ourselves and with each other, a different and a better way of being. These words are meant to celebrate the life of Jeni Gray and to honor the spirit in all of us that makes us one."

When Chester Whittle heard of the discovery of Jeni Gray's body, he again visited with his client in the small interview room at the Watauga County Jail. Again, it was a short visit with few words.

"They've found Jeni Gray," Whittle relayed to his client. "They found her in the area Leigh Cooper said they would find her."

"Yeah, I killed her and left her there. I sure did."

Incredulous, Whittle could not help but ask, "Why?"

The answer was given casually, "'Cause I wanted a piece of ass."

CHAPTER NINE

The Exposure

After the arrest of Daniel Lee, the Cooper family braced for whatever public reaction might ensue. They discussed how they would deal with their circumstances. Obviously, Leigh's testimony would be required to see that the criminal would pay for his crimes and be denied the opportunity to continue his ruthless ways.

The degree of painful exposure their daughter might receive during the trial of Daniel Lee was unknown to Louise and Claude; however, whatever the cost, all agreed that it would have to be paid. But the trial was then in the future, and there were immediate concerns. After a brief discussion, it was decided that the less said the better. Immediate family would be informed that Leigh had been assaulted. Specific questions would be answered, but only if asked. Information would not be volunteered outside of the family.

The plan seemed a good one. It offered a return to "normalcy" within the shortest possible time frame. However, even the best-laid plans often go awry—sometimes rather quickly. On Sunday morning, October 1, the *Winston-Salem Journal*, a regional newspaper, released a brief story reporting that, "Daniel Brian Lee of Triplett, North Carolina, was charged with sexual assault on a woman Saturday. He is accused of assaulting Leigh Martin Cooper of Boone." The next day the local *Watauga Democrat* printed a release with the specific charges in the case: "first degree sexual offense involving rape, first degree sexual offense involving oral intercourse, and first degree sexual offense involving anal intercourse."

Leigh Cooper accepted the release of the information better than her parents. After all, she said, "It *did* happen, and it *is* the truth."

Claude and Louise were concerned that their daughter was naïve to the ways of the world. They feared the consequences of the release of the information and its effect on people's attitudes toward Leigh. It was hard for them to understand how reporters and journalists could be so insensitive to the plight of a young person.

Louise cautioned Claude against doing anything rash. She reminded him they grew up in a world where "pregnant" was not a suitable word in polite company, and "sex" was a four-letter word. "The damage is done," she said. "People will understand," she said. "A harsh response will only draw attention to the information," she said. "The best thing to do is to remain calm and quiet," she said.

Louise sincerely believed her advice to her husband. She was therefore, surprised when she found herself in the front office of the *Watauga Democrat* the following day. She stated, to no one in particular but in a voice loud enough to be heard throughout the offices: "My name is Louise Cooper. I am the mother of Leigh Cooper. I want all of you to meet me. I want you to know that I am a real person, a person of flesh and blood. So is my daughter. She did not want what happened to her to happen. She's been through a lot. Thanks to you people, she's got a lot more to go through!"

The remarks brought the work of the newsroom to a halt. Everyone sat wide-eyed and stunned in the silence that followed. An employee tried to come to the defense of the paper, "Mrs. Cooper, we all sincerely regret what happened to your daughter. If we could have prevented it, I assure you we would have. But it is our duty to report the news. That's what we do. It is customary to release charges that are brought against alleged criminals. However, we did not release your daughter's name."

"No," Louise replied, "your journalistic counterparts in

Winston Salem did that. Between the two of you, very little was left to the imagination!" Louise turned and exited the office. A part of her was disappointed that she had failed to heed her own advice in regard to confronting the media; another part of her was damn well satisfied!

Joe Goodman, the managing editor of the *Winston-Salem Journal*, was spared the uncomfortable confrontation with the mother of the victim. But, had it occurred, it would not have been the first such event for Joe. His paper was one of relatively few papers across the country whose policy called for the release of rape victim's names. The policy was in opposition to conventional thinking, and had often served as a lightning rod for criticism of the paper. If it were not so fervently believed by the "Journal's" editors to be the correct policy, it would have been dropped for convenience long ago.

The policy did not result from inattention. It evolved from careful consideration concerning the basic tenets of journalism and justice. Goodman believed that the purpose of journalism was to report the news, to inform society of its location upon the continuum of maturity.

Goodman said, "We don't like to write about victims or victimization, but we're not public relations people, either. It is not our job to hide ugly things with pretty words. We still prefer 'garbage dump' to 'sanitary landfill.' We don't do euphemisms. We tell the truth. We name names."

On the justice side of the argument, it was clear to Goodman that the fairness of the system was based upon the right of the accused to be presumed innocent and allowed to face his accuser. Statistics showed that a significant number of those charged with rape were ultimately found not to be guilty. If fairness called for the release of the name of the accused, it must surely require the name of the accuser as well.

The idea that a sex crime was somehow "different" from other crimes of violence, wherein victim's names were routinely reported, seemed rooted in the belief that a rape victim was somehow "damaged goods." Failing to reveal rape victim's names would validate that old and outdated Victorian belief. Withholding names would perpetuate the very thing it would be striving to discourage.

A number of questions occurred to Mr. Goodman whenever he contemplated the potential public reaction to the release of a rape victim's name: Is it really reasonable to expect that people would sneer and view a victim as something less than she was before she was raped? Would normal individuals react in that manner? Would decent people, the ones whose respect counts, react in that manner? Could it not be assumed that society is somewhat better than that? Would not the withholding of the victim's name bespeak an editorial arrogance and disrespect for the maturity of the general public? Wouldn't we all be better off if rapists were viewed as the ones deserving of humiliation? Wouldn't there be fewer rapists if that happened?

And there was one other reason Mr. Goodman believed naming victims was appropriate. It concerned a widely diversified group that was often overlooked. He said, "What about the relatives, the associates, the neighbors, the casual acquaintances, the civic club compatriots, the church members, the classmates and friends that range from the postman to the pharmacist at the drugstore? They care. If left uninformed, they are denied the opportunity to express their compassion and concern or to offer their assistance and consolation."

Leigh Cooper's experiences seemed to support the editor's beliefs. Many calls and visits transpired at the Cooper home in the days following the rape. Of course, roommates and track teammates visited to demonstrate their support, but so did former roommates and other classmates and friends.

The steady stream of cards and flowers and fruit baskets lasted for weeks. Distant family members sent long letters expressing their concern and offering whatever assistance they might provide. They frequently spoke of their admiration for her ingenuity and persistence.

The maintenance man at Leigh's apartment complex read of her ordeal and immediately installed a deadbolt lock on the door to her apartment. The door already had a deadbolt; when he finished it had two.

Of particular interest were those good tidings which accrued from persons unknown to the family—friendship cards with nothing more than a signature, anonymous notes expressing admiration, letters of praise with unfamiliar signatures published in the local newspaper, flowers—many flowers!—often with no card whatsoever. And, as if to amplify the outpouring of compassion, the anticipated adverse reactions never came: no condescending attitudes, no ill will, no pity.

The most significant residue of her violation was Leigh Cooper's curiosity regarding her attacker. What could possibly cause one human being to treat others in such a way? She longed for answers regarding Daniel Lee.

CHAPTER TEN

The Villain

The murderer's full name was Daniel Brian Lee. After his arrest, it was a name that became synonymous with cruelty and perversion. It adorned the headlines of the newspapers of North Carolina for months.

The face that belonged to the name seemed appropriate. The arrest mug-shot accompanied the earliest newspaper articles. The face certainly appeared one that many might construe as that of a rapist and murderer: long, scraggily hair, beady eyes, weak chin, and shaggy, patchy beard. Another photo, taken as the accused was escorted to his arraignment, seemed to confirm every frightening thought of Daniel Lee as a demented and sub-human killer and rapist. The picture appeared on the front page of the local paper. With hands cuffed and long hair flowing in the breeze, he strode into the courthouse between the two bastions of local law enforcement, Chief Tester and Sherriff Lyons.

But Daniel Brian Lee was not always viewed as subhuman. He did not in the least appear a demented soul when he arrived in this world on May 22, 1966, weighing-in at a whopping six pounds, three ounces. On that day, he was viewed as a miracle, a somewhat late-arriving miracle, an unplanned miracle, but a miracle, nevertheless. Jacob Lee was forty-five years old when Daniel was born. His daughter, Sharon, was thirteen; daughter, Robin, was ten.

The Lees viewed their son with a similar degree of wonder and pride as Jeni Gray's parents experienced upon her arrival just four years previous. Daniel's sister Robin remembered, "Holding Daniel close was Mama's greatest joy. She

—Jamie Fletcher/ Democrat Staff
Suspect Daniel Brian Lee, who has been charged with the murder
of Jeni Gray, 27, of Boone, is escorted to a court appearance Tuesday
by Watauga County Sheriff Red Lyons (left) and
Police Chief R. Zane Tester.
(Appeared in the Watauga Democrat—October 11, 1989)

had longed for a son. She had pretty much raised two girls and she was an excellent mother to all of us, but she clearly had a special love for her little boy."

In nearly every instance, Daniel appeared a normal child. He crawled and walked within a normal timeframe. He was a small child who exhibited the typical traits of the young male of the species—a high level of activity and curiosity. His energy seemed to know no bounds.

Daniel was clearly a "Mama's boy." Mary Ellen Lee had a special affinity for her late-arriving little boy. During Daniel's early years, Mary Ellen's husband, Jacob, worked long hours in a key position within the military supply operation at Fort Bragg, in Fayetteville, North Carolina. The raising of the child was left almost entirely to his mother.

Daniel's favorite days as a youngster were those when his

mother and sisters would take him swimming. A day of frolic in the water, followed by a visit to the local fast-food chain for burgers and fries, was a day well spent indeed. It was even worth the drudgery of being dragged through the ordeal of shopping, which usually accompanied such otherwise pleasant outings.

This first day of school was not a good one for the boy. He was much more comfortable in the company of his two beagle puppies and under the protection of a devoted and doting mother than in the competitive school environment.

Jacob Lee declared his final retirement from government service in 1977. He moved his family to western North Carolina, where he purchased a house and land in the Triplett community in the rolling hills at the foot of the Blue Ridge Mountains. The move was a pleasant one for Daniel. He loved the natural beauty—clear, trout-filled streams, rugged forests, and mountains bathed in a hue of blue.

The boy developed a love for the people of the community. Long summer days were spent playing with the children of the closest neighbors. At the age of 12, he attempted to demonstrate his "manhood" by working many hours in the service of a family building a house down the road from his home.

And he assumed the duty, of his own accord, to check on and help Pearle Bishop, a neighbor whose husband's work called for him to be away during the week. He gathered wood, retrieved grocery items from the community store, carried out the trash, pulled weeds in the garden, and, generally, just looked after her as best he could. As did so many of the other residents of the community, Pearle only knew Daniel Lee as a kind, considerate, and respectful young man. It would never be possible for her to envision her young benefactor as a murderer devoid of humanity and compassion.

Daniel's troubles in school continued from elementary school into high school. Although of average intelligence, he always managed to under-perform and frustrate the expectations of his teachers. When he entered high school he joined the company of an unsavory group of friends and was introduced to alcohol and marijuana. He discovered that, particularly marijuana, provided an escape from the pressures of the outside world. Quietly, Daniel ceased to attend school at all.

Daniel Brian Lee
Watauga High School
yearbook, 1982

His desire for a means of transportation dictated a search for employment. He was hired as a dishwasher at Grandpa's Restaurant, and was eventually able to purchase a car. With his new-found freedom, he enrolled at Caldwell Community College, where he rather quickly obtained his General Education Development Certificate. That particular accomplishment offered a sweet taste of success. It led to a better job at a bigger restaurant, the Grandview, where he was given greater responsibility. The employees at the Grandview maintained a closeness that was new to Daniel. The regular customers treated the employees as friends. It was a supportive and rewarding atmosphere.

The upturn in his career was, unfortunately, paralleled by a nosedive in his life at home. His mother, his greatest friend and confidant, was slowly succumbing to the irreversible chokehold of emphysema. When not working, Daniel sat at her bedside. He shared the joyful news of his new friends and his love of his job with her. When she was awake, he comforted and encouraged her; when she slept, he held her hand and suffered with each tortured rise and fall of her breast.

To his everlasting regret, Daniel's mother passed away on February 11, 1987. Happily, for her, the last recall of her son was that of a young man on the rise, an individual who finally seemed to have found his direction. And, to all appearances, it was the right direction. He had a fragment of purpose, and he had friends.

Then, to top it all, at a party celebrating his twenty-first birthday, he met a girl—Janie Hunt. A divorcee, she was, at first, unimpressed with Daniel; however, he was smitten with her. He mounted an impressive campaign to win her favor. For a time, his shy and retiring attitude was shed as he struggled to gain the attention of his new friend of the female persuasion. He had the will; he found the way. Janie was gradually won over by the sincere and determined advances of her young suitor. She came to accept his admiration and developed a sincere appreciation for his desire to please her.

Daniel's feelings for Janie were evidenced via a note he left in her car one day when she was at work:

"Hello, Miss Janie! What's up? Not much here, just got the missing Janie blues. I wish we already had a place, but I guess that will happen pretty soon when I get my refund from the IRS. We'll get us a place and we'll get by with a real nice place. I just hope that will happen real soon. We need to find out how much a church wedding will cost I think. I'd like to have one of them instead of just going to the magistrate. If possible, let's get married as soon as we get a place. Does that sound all right to you? I guess that is all for now. I can't wait till I can see you again. I love you, Babe. I love you so much. I want us to be together all the time. I love you. Daniel."

Daniel and Janie agreed to see each other exclusively. She moved into the Lee household, where she shared Daniel's room in the back of the house at the head of the stairs. The couple circulated within a close-knit group of friends, mostly from the Grandview. Marriage plans were made. Life was good.

But then, on May 30, 1988, a weakness in the wall of a minute blood vessel in the brain of Daniel Lee led to a ballooning of a small portion of the vessel. Pressure from blood flow caused an infinitesimal rupture. A hole, smaller than the end of a fine point pen, allowed blood to escape into the cavity of the brain.

The importance of the tissues involved in the rupture was

illustrated by the length of the scientific names by which they are called. It was not by coincidence that such vital faculties were located deep in the center of the brain cavity, their critical functions insulated from shock and protected by the confining bony plate of the skull.

Pressure upon such vital components posed dire consequences. A variety of effects might have been anticipated, but some would be unexpected—and not fully understood. At approximately 9:30 p.m., while lying in the bed with Janie, Daniel experienced the first of the immediate effects of the injury to his brain: he was rocked by the most excruciating pain he had ever experienced. It was so intense that he passed immediately, but briefly, from consciousness. Within seconds the voluntary control of his bladder and bowels was lost. When his awareness of his surroundings returned, it was only partial and was clouded by the continuation of the pain. He fought to gain a hold on reality, but meandered in and out of consciousness as nonsense words flowed from his lips.

Daniel was taken by ambulance to Watauga County Medical Center, where his condition was found to be critical. He was rushed to Baptist Hospital in Winston Salem. There the quick action of a skilled surgeon relieved the pressure on his brain. Although his situation was still serious and his condition critical, the operation was deemed a success.

The patient's recuperation was viewed as remarkable. In a few short weeks Daniel was back at home and on his way to recovery. Five weeks after his surgery, he was deemed ready to return to work. Doctors were amazed that their patient seemed to have suffered absolutely no ill effects from his injury: no limp, no slurred speech, no drawn muscles, no loss of sensation—no apparent ill effects whatever.

"Apparent" can be a deceptive word. It is not a long word; but the importance of a single word cannot be measured in units of letters. Knowledgeable people, medical doctors, said no ill effects from the acute insult to Daniel Lee's brain were "apparent."

Not everyone agreed. In fact, some said the individual who returned home was not the one who was delivered to the hospital. Some contended the person transported died on the operating table, and the individual who was returned was a tormented beast.

CHAPTER ELEVEN

The Preliminaries

Chester Whittle, a well-known and highly respected local lawyer, was the appointed attorney for the indigent Daniel Lee. His law degree was from the University of Florida. He possessed and exuded a quality essential to the law: integrity. However, "duty" was the word that best described Whittle's assignment to the case of Daniel Lee. When a judicial authority circulated a letter pointing out that an insufficient number of attorneys were sharing the responsibilities of indigent cases in the region, Chester volunteered. He did his duty. His reward was the assignment to defend Daniel Lee.

Duty was not a stranger to Chester Whittle; he had paid its price before. During the Vietnam conflict, he believed it was the duty of young men to serve their country. He did his duty. He went; he served; luckily, he survived. Many did not. He was never quite sure what was gained by his service or their sacrifice.

The statutes of the State of North Carolina allowed for two defenders in capital offense cases. Whittle asked young attorney, Jeff Hedrick, a relatively recent graduate of the University of North Carolina School of Law, to assist with the defense of Daniel Lee. Hedrick, like Whittle, was born to the law; his father was the Chief Judge of the North Carolina Court of Appeals. Hedrick proved to be an invaluable member of the team for the defense.

During Mr. Whittle's first visit with Daniel Lee after he was assigned the case, he introduced himself and listened as his client denied any wrong-doing in regard to Leigh Cooper, Jeni Gray or anyone else. The prisoner claimed he failed to understand why he was in jail.

Whittle began, "Mr. Lee, I am not yet aware of the full magnitude of the charges against you. It appears, at the least, you are to be charged with kidnapping and rape. I am your court-appointed attorney, and I intend to defend you to the best of my ability against whatever charges may come. However, the court does not require me to endure sitting in this small room with you smelling the way you do. I'm going to gather as much information as I can about the legal charges you're facing, and you're going to get a nice, long shower before we meet again. Do you understand that?"

"Yes, sir."

As the seriousness of the charges became apparent to Daniel Lee's attorneys and as they were gradually made aware of the depth and breadth of the evidence supporting the charges, meetings with their client became more frequent. Whittle and Hedrick thoroughly explained to the defendant the charges he faced and the possible penalties to be enforced if he were to be convicted. They were amazed at the lack of concern their client exhibited regarding the entire situation. The attorneys were only made aware of the seriousness of their client's aneurysm and the subsequent changes in his behavior through conversations with family members and neighbors.

Whittle and Hedrick initiated contact with medical professionals at Baptist Hospital to corroborate the serious nature of the medical problem experienced by Daniel Lee, and launched a search to find the best neuropsychiatrist available to investigate the defendant's behavior. Both efforts produced positive results and offered some hope of understanding the defendant's actions.

Before the trial could begin, the court had to first determine if Daniel Lee was competent to stand trial at all. Professionals at Dorothea Dix Hospital in Raleigh were retained to examine Mr. Lee and ascertain whether he was able to meet the two primary criteria imposed by the law: Was he capable of understanding the charges against him? Was he capable of cooperating in his own defense? The evaluation, which took two weeks to complete, concluded the defendant met both criteria.

After the discovery of Jeni Gray's body, the defendant's attorneys informed him that the tremendous weight of evidence related to his guilt rendered negligible the prospects for a finding of "not guilty" at trial. They pointed out that a guilty plea might beget special consideration in sentencing: certain inflammatory evidence might not be introduced at a sentencing hearing that would be routinely included at a regular trial, and factors related to his mental condition might stand as worthy mitigating factors for a jury to consider. The defendant decided to plead guilty.

A guilty plea in this case did not remove the necessity of a trial. The capital sentencing statute of North Carolina decreed that any evidence received during the guilt phase of a trial was competent evidence for the jury to hear in the sentencing phase. Clearly, the prosecution wanted to make known to the jury the horrendous nature of the crimes, and the defense wished to reveal any mitigating factors that were found to exist before a sentence was handed down.

The defense believed their client could not receive a fair trial in Watauga County due to the degree of unfavorable, pre-trial publicity that had been distributed. When the motion for a change in venue was made, a number of prominent local citizens submitted affidavits attesting to the belief that, due to the gruesome nature of the crime, the magnitude of the negative publicity, and the popularity of the victim, it would be very difficult for the defendant to obtain a fair trial in Watauga County. The judge agreed and granted a change of venue to neighboring Avery County. The change was not a "win" for the defense as Avery County had been exposed to a similar amount of negative publicity. Plus, the citizens of Avery were often considered even more conservative than those of Watauga County.

In a pre-trial motion, the defense sought to suppress the sharing of photographs of the victim with the jury. Mr. Whittle appealed, "Your Honor, these pictures are just not necessary. They are gruesome, and the probative value is not outweighed by the unfairly prejudicial consequences that will result from their viewing. And, Your Honor, that showing of her full, nude body—well, I think it's uncalled for. I mean, showing her privates and all. Wouldn't a verbal description suffice under the circumstances? A significant measure of the damage to the body is the result of the elements and the animals and the insects. These photographs could confuse the jury. They were taken fifteen days after the murder. The prejudicial nature of these pictures is such that they should not be admitted. "

The District Attorney responded: "Well, Judge, I'm sorry but the crime was gruesome. And it would seem to me that it's very relevant to show the body at the location where the body was found. Now, we have eliminated photographs that are duplicitous. Those we have submitted show the body from different angles, and we contend they are admissible to support the testimony of the witnesses who will attest to its condition."

"The motion to exclude is overruled," the Judge declared. "The pictures are in. Let's move on."

From the final summary for the State of North Carolina:

"Wasn't it amazing when defense counsel implied that the condition of the victim's body was the result of exposure to the elements and the activity of the woodland animals and insects? I am very confident that such tactics cannot fool you, ladies and gentlemen of the jury. You know that there is but one cause for the condition of that precious body. There is no other force, no other being, no other entity, responsible for the condition of that body other than Mr. Daniel Lee. He killed her and he left her out there in that wilderness! Animals would not have torn her flesh, the elements would not have ravaged her remains, had she never come into contact with this villain!"

Of course, the motion related to the BBs discovered in Jeni Gray's vagina was addressed, and the inability to determine if the victim was dead or alive at the time of the incident required the court to exclude the evidence. The ruling was certainly a favorable one for the defense.

The jousting for legal position going into the trial was finally at an end. Whittle and Hedrick had worked hard to set the stage for the best possible outcome for their client: life imprisonment. They would contend and attempt to convince the jury that, since the medical problems experienced by their client could not be ruled out as the cause of his actions, it would be unconscionable to take his life.

The District Attorney would have none of that.

CHAPTER TWELVE
The State

District Attorney, Tom Rusher, had little doubt as to the appropriate punishment for Daniel Lee. The death penalty was not cruel nor was it unusual to Tom. He firmly believed that certain crimes warranted its application. Rusher was aware that life imprisonment almost never translated to *imprisonment for life* in North Carolina. In fact, to his knowledge, the longest anyone had remained incarcerated in the state was less than thirty years. If Daniel Lee served thirty years, he would still be eleven years short of retirement age when released. That was unacceptable to the District Attorney.

Rusher was a student of the law and its history in the northwest mountain region. He often referred to the story of Reed Coffey of Avery County. Years ago, Mr. Coffey shot a deputy sheriff through the kitchen window as the lawman sat at the table with his family. The murderer was given the death sentence, but the Governor later commuted the sentence to life imprisonment. Coffey was released after serving twelve years. His final days passed peacefully. He died of natural causes.

The story was believed by some to present a shining example of the appropriateness of life imprisonment over the death penalty—of allowing individuals to pay their fair debt to society. Tom Rusher wondered about the fairness to the victim's family. They, too, had debts, not debts to society but the type of debts society does not forgive—to the Savings and Loan, the bank, and the tax collector. And they were left without a father, a husband, a provider.

Rusher understood how it happened that life sentences were commuted. As time passed, "bleeding hearts" entered the fray; loved ones of the victim died-off or would just try to forget the tragic circumstances; overcrowded conditions called for the release of prisoners, and it was only logical to consider first those who had been incarcerated the longest. Tom understood why it happened; he just didn't believe it should.

Rusher determined to use his twenty years of experience, nine years as Assistant District Attorney and eleven as the headman for the 24th Judicial District, to pursue the death penalty in the most aggressive manner. His record in regard to the death penalty was impressive. He had obtained convictions for first-degree murder in seven North Carolina counties.

The District Attorney's business was serious, and he was serious about it. His success as a prosecutor was not the result of style or finesse; it stemmed from his "bull-dog" tenacity and commitment to hard work. Tom seldom smiled, which was a pity, for his smile was handsome and brightened his face.

He was not without a sense of humor, a sense of humor that sometimes surfaced in his work. In one murder trial, the accused claimed that the gun he had pointed at an innocent person's face "just to scare him" had mysteriously discharged of its own accord: "I didn't pull the trigger. I didn't shake the gun. I didn't do nothin'!" said the shooter. "It just fired on its own! When that happened, I shoved it in my belt and ran."

"So," responded Rusher, "you would have us believe, sir, that you took this weapon, this pistol with a mind of its own, this revolver that fires without warning or assistance and without cause, and you shoved it into your pants—pointed directly at your own genitals!—and you entrusted your private parts to the whim and fancy of this independent and unpredictable weapon as you hastily made your retreat. Is that your testimony, sir?"

"Well, not exactly the way you put it," came the barely audible response.

Gerry (Gerald) Wilson, Rusher's associate for the preceding nine years, would ably assist the prosecution. Wilson was an excellent prosecutor in his own right—one of the best in the state; however, he was capable, seemingly in an instant, of becoming an extraordinary support person. His ability to shift from the role of Captain to that of First Mate, and to perform those duties with a flourish, was a great asset to the prosecution.

The Judge for the trial of Daniel Lee was the Honorable Charles Lamm. Originally a "flatlander" from the little town of Wilson in eastern North Carolina, Lamm had come under the spell of the ancient mountains of the Blue Ridge where he resided. He was respected and admired by the people of the region. He enjoyed the confidence of his peers on the bench, and was highly regarded by legal minds throughout the state.

An asset Lamm brought to the court was that of decisiveness. He did not vacillate. He was consistent in his opinions and constant in his application of the law. He believed trials should move along at a brisk pace, and that they should begin as soon as practicable. Jury selection in the trial of Daniel Lee was accomplished expeditiously and was uneventful. On April 15, 1990, Judge Lamm alerted the District Attorney, "Mr. Rusher, I will ask for your opening statement and the beginning of the presentation of the evidence for the State tomorrow morning."

CHAPTER THIRTEEN
The Prosecution

O h yes, oh yes, oh yes. This court is now open and sitting for the dispatch of its business. God save the State and this honorable Court: The Honorable Charles C. Lamm, Judge presiding."
  —Sheriff Clinton Phillips, Avery County, N.C., April 16, 1990

An air of excitement surrounded the beginning of the trial of Daniel Lee. Media attention from five states was focused on the little courthouse in Newland, North Carolina. The news of the B.B.'s found in the body of Jeni Gray had leaked and spread like wildfire. It singled out the case as one with particularly gruesome dimensions; and, consequently, one of great interest. Local residents were thrilled to see, in person, the news personalities they viewed on television each evening. Youngsters walked behind live interviews on the courthouse lawn and waved to the cameras. They returned home and waited anxiously to see themselves on the evening news.

On the morning of the first day of the trial, the participants were busily engaged in their appropriate activities. Mr. Rusher appeared as stern and serious as ever as he discussed final preparations with his associate, Mr. Wilson. Chester Whittle was, of course, relaxed. He exchanged pleasantries with his co-counsel and perused his notes.

The first surprise of the day was a big one, and it came early. When the defendant was led into the courtroom, a murmur fluttered across the gallery. Newspaper photographs and articles had conjured a frightening vision of the accused in the minds of the assembled. The reality was in stark contrast to the expectation. The defendant appeared much more a docile lamb than a savage beast. He seemed to have undergone a reverse metamorphosis. His manner was subdued— even skittish. Shorn of his mask of scraggly hair and stripped of his armor of dirt and grime, he was a pitiful excuse of a villain. He wore a white shirt, khaki pants, and a frightened look. A word went right to the heart of his appearance. It was an ironic word—"innocent." He just looked innocent. Not "innocent" as in "blameless" or "free from guilt" but "innocent" as in "simple," "unknowing," or "childlike." However, an innocent individual does not plead guilty to a merciless killing.

Mr. Rusher bellowed for the court, "What say you, Mr. Daniel Lee, are you guilty of first degree murder as you are charged in the Bill of Indictment, or are you not guilty?"

Lee replied softly but distinctly, "Guilty."

"Have you been provided with a copy of the first-degree murder statute, and has it been explained to you?" asked Judge Lamm.

"Yes, sir."

When the acceptance of the plea was completed, it was time for the sentencing hearing to begin. Judge Lamm called on Mr. Rusher to begin his presentation on behalf of the state.

Note: The prosecution of Daniel Lee was led by longtime District Attorney Tom Rusher with the capable assistance of future District Attorney, Gerald Wilson. Comments from the final summary for the prosecution have been presented in bold type previously in this account and will continue to be presented at appropriate and proximate times throughout the book. Dialogue is taken from the trial transcript except in instances where information was added to facilitate transition and/or understanding of the testimony.

The defense of Daniel Lee was a joint effort of attorney Chester Whittle and his valued colleague, Jeff Hedrick. Comments from the final summary for the defense are introduced and presented in bold, italic type to distinguish them from those of the prosecution. Again, dialogue was lifted from the trial transcripts with minor changes or additions to facilitate transitions and clarity.

Rusher responded to Judge Lamm, "Thank you, Your Honor. May it please the Court, ladies and gentlemen of the jury, you have been carefully selected; and that's the way it should be. You have each stated that you will be fair and you will be impartial, and I'm confident of that. As you have heard from the beginning, I am an advocate for a cause; and I have the benefit of the entire investigation that has taken place in regard to this case."

The District Attorney then provided an overview for the jury of what the prosecution's evidence would show. He maintained that, although some of the evidence might be imprecise, such as the exact location of Ms. Gray's abduction, the fact of her abduction and the horrors she was forced to endure were well documented. He detailed the extent of the victim's injuries. Emphasis was given to the fact that the defendant was engaged in a course of action, which included kidnapping, raping, and killing young women.

The District Attorney's opening remarks ended thusly: "Now ladies and gentlemen, we're going to show you the evidence, and we're going to be contending that this case is an aggravated one beyond any and all reasonable doubt. You will come to know and understand, after the presentation of our evidence, that there is but one appropriate punishment for Mr. Daniel Brian Lee. I sincerely believe you will agree with the State that the death penalty was created for just such as he."

The prosecution then began the presentation of an avalanche of evidence. Jeni Gray's roommate testified to her recollection of the events of the morning of her disappearance. Bob Gray told of the plans he had to meet with his daughter. Police Officer Tom Redmond described the search efforts engaged in by the police and the sense of urgency that surrounded the efforts.

Officer Luther Harrison was an important witness for the prosecution. He carried the banner of local law enforcement, the banner of the investigation. He mounted the witness stand with a huge book under his arm. The book contained detailed information related to every facet of the investigation. It recorded facts and events; it documented places, times, people and conditions. The book was the culmination of the painstaking labor of every member of the law enforcement community. With confidence and pride and at the direction of the District Attorney, Officer Harrison shared the results of the investigation with the jury.

Dr. John Butts was called to the stand to report the results of the autopsy he had performed on the body of Jeni Gray. At the request of the District Attorney, the noted pathologist described in detail the extent of the injuries the victim sustained. When the blows to the head were addressed, the District Attorney inquired, "Doctor, would those blows have been painful?"

"Well, of course."

"All of them, each and every one?"

"Certainly."

"Thank you, doctor."

As the facts surrounding his daughter's death were shared with the jurors, Bob Gray sat in the back of the courtroom with his arms folded across his chest. Beth, Jeni's stepmother, cried softly and continually beside him. His brow furrowed from time to time as he listened to others speak of his daughter's fate. Bob's face was framed with a well-groomed beard; it was a kindly, weathered, and now bewildered face.

As the activities of the court continued, Mr. Gray's attention honed in on Daniel Lee's family members—the father and the sister. What were they thinking? They sat meekly, apologetically, as if they wished not to occupy any space at all. Jacob Lee stared vacantly at the floor; his daughter continually patted his knee with one hand and brushed away tears—hers and her father's—with the other hand.

Curiously, as he gazed across the room, the thought occurred to Mr. Gray: Would I rather be sitting where I sit or across the room? Would I rather be the father of the victim or the murderer? Inwardly, he laughed at himself. What a choice? And what a silly supposition? But the thought provided more than a little comfort, for in his heart, Bob knew the answer to the question. He would rather be right where he was. He had lost a beautiful and beloved daughter, but he retained pleasant memories of her gentle spirit. The Lees, on the other hand, had just as assuredly lost—whether through the humiliation of enforced extermination or via an agonizing and never-ending confinement—a son and a brother. Now loyalty demanded that they sit behind a shadowy figure that bore only a vague resemblance to the one they once knew and loved.

The terrific irony of the situation suddenly became apparent to Bob. His family and that of Daniel Lee had a great deal in common. They were inextricably linked, for they shared—albeit from different perspectives—a common tragedy. In fact, they probably had a closer real affinity than any other persons in the courtroom: together, they knew a deep and abiding, gnawing pain.

When the afternoon recess was called, T.V. cameras followed Bob Gray to the lobby of the courthouse to capture the image of a father who had just heard graphic testimony relating to the last moments of his daughter's life. They were surprised to record an unexpected scene as the father of the victim strolled directly to the father of the murderer. Mr. Gray took a wide-eyed Jacob Lee by the hand and said softly, "Mr. Lee, I'm Bob Gray, and I want you to know that I bear you no malice. I understand this is very hard on you, too. We will all have to do our best to get through it. It's all we can do."

Mr. Lee's eyes filled with tears. He could only summon the strength to say, "Thank you, sir. Thank you very much." Mr. Lee's daughter, Robin Lee Daniels, extended her hand to Mr. Gray. She could not speak but her eyes conveyed a sincere appreciation for the kind gesture.

When court resumed, the parade of witnesses for the prosecution continued: Donnie Farmer described the discovery of Jeni's body; Deputy Collins told of the rainy trip to Triplett, North Carolina, and the arrest of Daniel Lee; Robert Melton reported the results of the meticulous search and cataloging of evidence found in the defendant's car; John Stubbs relayed his findings at the crime scene; David Spittle conveyed the blood sample analysis from the club found at the crime scene and the athletic shoes recovered from the defendant's home (and yes, the expert in the area of forensic serology, the study of bodily fluids, was named Spittle); Wayne Bendure detailed the incriminating evidence discovered via his exhaustive fiber sample comparisons; Scott Worsham revealed the successful findings concerning correlating hair samples; Agent Steve Wilson confirmed that the underwear discovered at the Lee home was identical to that worn by Leigh Cooper on the night she was raped.

Finally, due to the lateness of the hour on the trial's third day, the crush of the evidence was paused. Judge Lamm called for the hearing to resume at 10 a.m. the following morning. Only one witness remained for the prosecution, but she was the most important witness of all: Leigh Cooper.

Leigh sat alone in the living room of her parent's home on the night prior to her appearance as a trial witness. She rested on the couch and stared out the window. Lost in thought, she did not realize her father had entered the room and seated himself in the chair at her side. Claude cleared his throat and asked, "And what is my girl so absorbed in thought about?"

"I was just thinking about tomorrow, that's all."

"You know, honey, I'm not so sure tomorrow is necessary anymore. I mean, he's pled guilty. A lot has changed since you first committed to do this. You don't really have to testify."

"But, I do. I really do. You know I've never been embarrassed by any of this."

Claude cautioned, "You say that now, but you might not always feel that way."

"Maybe not, but I hope I will. I hope I always remember that the shame is his. He earned it; he owns it; I want him to have it. I think he counted on me being embarrassed, on me hiding and being afraid the rest of my life. Don't you see? That's why he just went home and didn't run. He counted on me being too afraid to tell. Well, he got the wrong girl.

"I want to do this because I want him to see that I'm fine physically; but more, I want him to know that I'm fine mentally and emotionally. I want him to see for himself. Tomorrow, I'm going to walk up to that stand and tell the God's truth. I won't be embarrassed, or vengeful, or happy, or sad. I'll just be me. And he'll see that I'm just unaffected by what he did. Maybe he won't understand; maybe his brain really is screwed up. But if it is, then it won't matter anyway. If it's all an act though, he will understand. If he can understand, I want him to know that he didn't do what he set out to do. And I want women everywhere who have ever been violated, or ever will be violated, to know that it's not their fault and the people who matter will support them just like you and Mom and Chris and all those other people have supported me. And I damn sure don't want him to get away with what he did to Jeni Gray."

The next morning Mr. Rusher's voice rang out, "The State calls Leigh Martin Cooper to the stand."

Leigh was the very essence of youth and health as she confidently approached the witness stand and was sworn to the truth—"God's truth."

Rusher began slowly. His very general and carefully worded questions provided considerable latitude for the witness to convey her story. She was poised and self-assured as she carried both the jury and the gallery with her to the lonely and dark Jake's Mountain Road. A deep and pervasive silence settled on the courtroom as the witness reported the rapist's question, "Do you want a slow death or a fast death?"

After the trial, Mr. Whittle would say, "You know, with everyone looking up at Leigh Cooper on the elevated witness

Leigh Martin Cooper, 1989

stand in that old courtroom, she seemed suspended in the air. She glowed like an angel. Hell, she is an angel! What defense can deal with that?"

With the completion of the testimony of the State's star witness, Mr. Rusher declared, "I have no further questions, your Honor, and that concludes the case for the prosecution."

The defense attorneys looked to each other in dismay after Leigh Cooper's testimony. They knew her testimony would be damaging, but it was even more impactful than they had imagined. It was painfully clear the mitigating factors the defense might present would have to be considerable indeed; for the jury, at that point, surely accepted the accuracy of Mr. Rusher's introductory statement: "The death penalty was created for just such as Daniel Brian Lee!"

CHAPTER FOURTEEN
The Defense

The day after the conclusion of the case for the prosecution, Judge Lamm called for Mr. Whittle to commence his presentation for the defense. Whittle's opening remarks began: "May it please the Court, ladies and gentlemen of the jury, this case is not a pleasant one. In a word, it is gruesome. Gratefully, there are a lot of things you won't have to guess about or speculate about with this case. You are not being asked to determine guilt—that would be superfluous. Guilt has already been admitted. Your duty is to decide upon an appropriate punishment. I don't believe that point can be overemphasized: there is no doubt that this boy is guilty; the question is, what punishment fits the crime? You must decide to what degree the crime is an aggravated one, and whether or not there exist circumstances that mitigate the severity of any aggravating factors found to exist.

"The goal of the defense in this case is not the avoidance of punishment altogether; punishment is certainly called for. The defense will show, however, that considerable mitigating factors are present in this case. And these factors will raise, may I say, more than the reasonable doubt that is required to prohibit the imposition of the death penalty."

Whittle forecast what his evidence would show: Witnesses would confirm the defendant was a normal and loving individual prior to the occurrence of an aneurysm in his brain. The defense would show that the injury resulted in a drastic change in the defendant's behavior and ultimately led to the commission of the terrible crimes with which he was charged. Competent medical professionals would verify the existence of and the extent of the injuries to the defendant's brain.

Mr. Whittle's introductory comments concluded thusly, "Decent society should be protected from a brain damaged individual such as Daniel Lee, for such crimes should never be allowed to be repeated. However, this boy is not deserving of the death penalty. The defense contends that the appropriate punishment for this crime is life imprisonment. I trust that, after the facts are made known to you, you will agree. Thank you."

From the final summary for the State of North Carolina:

"I wish to remind you if I may, ladies and gentlemen of the jury, that we are considering here today the proper punishment for the 'man' Daniel Brian Lee. You may have noted that defense counsel sometimes refers to the 'boy,' Daniel Lee. You should know that we're both speaking of the same person. I suppose the defense refers to him as a 'boy' to gain your sympathy. I anticipate that counsel will refer to this murderer as a 'boy' in his final arguments.

"However, I wish to point out that by every generally accepted definition of which I am aware, the defendant is a 'man.' He is not a child. He is twenty-four years old. He is old enough to buy and consume alcoholic beverages; he is old enough to drive a car; he is old enough to vote, he is old enough to enter into contracts. He is, in all legal respects, a completely mature adult. I submit to you that adults should be treated and referred to as adults. They should not be referred to as 'boys.' "

From the final summary for the defense of Daniel Lee:

"The district attorney is thorough and relentless, isn't he? He gives no quarter. Why he even protested my referring to Daniel Lee as a 'boy.' He was so afraid some advantage might be gained. Well, the truth is, I have never really considered how I was referring to Daniel. However, since the very first time I talked to him, he has not seemed a 'man' to me. He does not seem to possess even the most rudimentary awareness that any mature 'man' has. He clearly does not

understand that one person cannot force another to say 'I love you' and have it be so."

The defense called Mr. Gordon Sox as its first witness. Mr. Sox, was a neighbor of the Lee family in Triplett, North Carolina.

Mr. Whittle asked, "What was your general opinion of Daniel as he was growing up, Mr. Sox?"

"Well, he was a good boy. He treated people with respect. He played with my children and visited in our house; my children visited with Daniel over at Jake's place, too. I remember Jake brought Daniel over and they helped when we were repairing an old building for a firehouse for the community. Daniel helped with whatever needed doing. He was a big help, and he got along with everyone. To my knowledge he was never violent, and I never heard anyone say he did anything violent."

"Mr. Sox, do you remember the night of May 30, 1988?"

"Yes, I do. I'm a member of the Watauga County Rescue Squad, and that night I picked up a call on the scanner at my home. In fact, the emergency was reported to be at Jacob Lee's house, which is just out the road from my home. I hurried out there and ran in the house through the open front door. I called out and got an answer from the back and up the stairs. I ran up the stairs and found Jake sitting on the bed with his arms around his son.

"Daniel didn't have any clothes on at that time, and he was just sort of limp in Jake's arms. But that didn't last long, for then he got a wild look in his eyes and he grabbed his head and started screaming at the top of his lungs. He began throwing himself around; why, it was all Jake and I could do to hold him down. The pain must have been excruciating. I was afraid at one point he was going to go right out the window and take me and Jake with him. But then, again, he would calm down and fall limp.

"I looked around the room, and it was a mess. Daniel had lost all control of his bowels and his bladder, and that bothered him quite a bit. When the pain would ease up, he'd look around, and he was obviously concerned about that. But then another pain would come, and we'd be back to trying to hold him down again. Finally, the rescue squad arrived, and, in between his spells, we were able to get him down the stairs and on a stretcher. They took him to the hospital."

"When did you next see Daniel, Mr. Sox."

"It was a long time after the incident, several months I'd say. My wife and I visited over at Jake's a couple of times after Daniel came home from the hospital, but he never came down from his room. Jake said he stayed up in his room nearly all the time. Finally, I did see him driving his car down the road. He gave a sort of half-wave, not a friendly wave like he used to. And his appearance changed over time. His hair grew long and it looked dirty. He quit shaving. His general appearance just seemed to deteriorate."

Whittle excused Mr. Sox, "Thank you, sir. That's all I have."

The next witness for the defense was the defendant's sister, Robin Lee Daniels. Robin was the single parent of a young daughter; she worked as an assistant medical librarian at the Watauga Medical Center. She testified her brother was a "typical little boy" when he was young. He loved his dogs and he took care of them. When Robin divorced, Daniel hauled her back home from Ohio and allowed her and her daughter to share his room at the head of the stairs in the Lee home until she could find a place of her own. Daniel voluntarily slept on the couch.

Daniel shared his dreams in late-night talk sessions with his sister. She testified, "He wanted to learn more about food preparation and the restaurant business. He hoped someday to own a restaurant of his own."

"Tell us what you remember about Daniel after his surgery, Robin."

"He wanted to stay in and rest all the time, which at first I figured was normal. But then it just seemed his energy was never going to come back. Even after he started back to work he would just come home and flop down. He was just zapped. And he seemed to take no interest in anything. He didn't talk about his ambitions anymore. He said he didn't want to take any more classes or anything. He stopped caring about his appearance and the appearance of his car and his room. He used to keep his room neat and tidy, and he was really fastidious about his records being kept in their covers. But after he came home his room was a complete mess.

"And his physical appearance really changed. Of course, the scar from the surgery was prominent, but he let his hair grow long and he didn't wash it. He stopped shaving and grew a scruffy beard. He stopped bathing; and, well, he just smelled bad."

"Did you discuss these things with him?"

"Yes, sir, but it didn't do any good. He just ignored me."

"Robin, to your knowledge, was Daniel ever violent?"

"No, sir. Never."

Daniel Lee's father, Jacob Lee, appeared feeble when he took the stand for the defense. He described himself as widowed with three children. He stated his age as "sixty-nine-year-old." He appeared older. Jacob confirmed the testimony of his daughter and Mr. Sox pertaining to Daniel being a normal and a "good" boy. He said his son liked to fish and hike in the mountains, and, in particular, he liked to cook.

When Mr. Whittle asked about Daniel's behavior after his surgery, Mr. Lee responded, "Well, I know he didn't eat like he should. And he got real quiet. He stayed in bed a lot, 'cause he didn't have any energy. He didn't want to cook anymore. And he just stopped taking care of his car and keepin' his room clean. His looks went downhill, too. He quit combin' his hair and shinin' his shoes. He just quit carin' it seemed."

"Did you notice anything about his bathing habits?"

"Well, no. That was none of my business. He stayed pretty much up in his room and kept to himself. I tried not to get onto him about things. The doctors told me that he could have a normal life. They said it would take time for him to get back to normal. I didn't want to cause him any problems by jumpin' on him about stuff, so I just let things go. I figured his health was more important at the time."

"Did you ever, sir, up until the time of these crimes, did you ever witness any violent behavior in your boy?"

"No."

"Mr. Lee, is Daniel the same young man he was before the aneurysm?"

"No, sir, he ain't the same boy at all."

"That's all I have of you, Mr. Lee."

Janie Carol Hunt, who was once Daniel Lee's fiancée, was then called to the stand. In response to Mr. Whittle's questions, Janie shared that she met Daniel at a party on May 29, 1987. Soon they began to see each other regularly. He brought her presents and flowers. He often helped with the cleaning of her house or prepared dinner while she cleaned. He sent her notes and cards declaring his affection. Ms. Hunt painted a vivid picture of blossoming love. In less than a year's time, Daniel proposed marriage and she accepted. While the planning continued and in order to reduce expenses, Janie moved into the Lee home with Daniel and his father. The couple began looking for a mobile home they would park on Mr. Lee's land. All was going well right up to the time of the aneurysm.

"Janie, can you tell us what you remember about Daniel's recovery from the surgery?"

"I saw him about midday the day after they operated. He looked real good. I mean, his head had been shaved and he had the incision, but his color was good. And he was real cheerful; he wanted to get up and go home. But the next day was a different story. His head was all swollen. His eye was swollen shut and turned black. He looked really bad. He was in the hospital about two and a half weeks.

"When he got home, his progress was real slow. He didn't want to do anything. He wouldn't eat. He always wanted to keep the shade down in his room. I kept tryin' to tell him he needed to get up and get out."

"In what ways did his behavior change, Janie?"

"Well, he began to be afraid of insects, bugs and spiders and things like that. They terrified him. For instance, if he killed a spider, he would say that all the rest of the spiders was goin' to come and get him. That's why he kept the flashlight with him in the bed. And he also had a B.B. gun and a can of insect spray with him. And he wouldn't sleep on the backside of the bed anymore, the side next to the wall. He said if somethin' was to get after him he wanted to be able to get out."

Janie described other changes in her fiancée: he had difficulty sleeping and played the stereo late into the night. His tastes in music changed; he abandoned the easy listening he loved for heavy-metal. He essentially stopped bathing and shaving to the degree that he looked rough and smelled worse. Basically, she said, "He just withdrew from life."

"How about his attitudes toward love and sex, Janie? Did they change, too?"

"He ordered some pornography tapes, and he watched them—a lot! And his carin' and givin' ways was not there anymore. He only wanted to satisfy himself. He started asking me to have anal sex with him, and I wouldn't do that. And then he ordered this life-size, blow-up doll with female parts. That did it for me. I left."

"When was the last time you saw Daniel before his arrest for these terrible crimes?"

"Oh, I guess it was about two months before he was arrested. I ran into him in town, and he really shocked me. I mean, his hair was flyin' back and I'm like—oh, my God! He didn't even look like Daniel anymore. He was a mess. He asked me for his engagement ring back, but then he said I could keep it if I would go to his house and have sex with him. I just left him standin' there and went on up the street."

"Just one more thing, Janie. Was Daniel ever violent with you or do you know of any time he was violent?"

"No, sir."

"Those are my questions, your Honor."

Mr. Wilson's booming voice was then heard throughout the courtroom: "Ms. Hunt, despite what you said, Mr. Lee and yourself did not have a particularly good relationship even before he became ill, now did you?"

"That's not right. We did."

"Do you recall in October of last year, speaking with Agent Wilson and Detective Harrison at the police station and telling them that you did not want to get serious with Daniel Lee? Do you recall that?"

"I didn't when I first met him."

"But then you said he got serious and bought you an engagement ring? Isn't that what you told them?"

"Yes."

"You said you had thought about marrying Lee, but he was just not the type of person that you wanted to marry. Don't you recall telling them that, Ms. Hunt?"

"No. I don't."

"And further, you had been trying to break off the relationship with Daniel Lee even before he gave you the ring, do you recall telling them that? And that the reason you didn't want to get involved with him or marry him was because he was so self-centered and childish, didn't you tell them all of that?"

"He wasn't that way before!"

"Well, then, what you told them was wrong. Is that what you're saying now, Ms. Hunt?"

"If that's what they said I told them, then it was wrong."

"Before the aneurysm or any of that business, you and Mr. Lee actually got into a physical fight out at the Grandview Restaurant, didn't you, Ms. Hunt? Slapped each other around a bit, didn't you?"

"Yes."

"He was drinking that day, wasn't he?"

"I slapped Daniel, and he slapped me back."

"Answer the question! Was he drinking or was he not?"

"Yes."

"But, Ms. Hunt, you testified a moment ago that the defendant had never been violent. You said he was always considerate toward you. But now I hear you say he was violent, and he was inconsiderate. So, which is it?"

"To me, that was an automatic reaction. It was not an act of violence!"

"To slap you is not an act of violence? I see. Ms. Hunt before Mr. Lee had his medical problems, he had 'girly' magazines, *Playboy* and others, now didn't he?"

"He didn't cut the pictures out of them!"

"Oh, I see. He only started cutting the pictures out later. Isn't it the truth that you never wanted to marry Daniel Lee? You viewed him as a self-centered, childish person, and you just finally broke off the relationship. Isn't that the truth of the matter?"

"After the aneurysm, he was, and I did break it off then."

Mr. Wilson concluded his cross examination: "That's all I have of her, your Honor."

From the final summary for the State of North Carolina:

"Let's remember that defense counsel claimed he would show that a 'drastic' change—not an insignificant change but a 'drastic' change—took place in Daniel Lee after the aneurysm. Well, I wish to ask, where are these witnesses who will report a 'drastic' change?

"What did you, members of the jury, hear? You heard he let his hair grow long. That's a 'drastic' change? Why many people do that. There's an entire industry dependent upon the fact that people like to change their hairstyles. Can that be considered as some sort of serious evidence of a change in attitude that led to murder?

"You heard that at some point in time his hygienic habits changed. He didn't wash as often as some people thought he should. People said they could smell him. Well, I thought it interesting that his own father didn't know anything about that. And I assure you, ladies and gentlemen of the jury, Daniel Lee

didn't stink Jeni Gray to death; he bludgeoned her with a club and then he choked her to death!

"Now the defendant's girlfriend—or the woman who says she was his girlfriend—said he never demonstrated any violent tendencies with her. However, she failed to recall that Mr. Lee had once struck her in the face in a public restaurant. You will remember it was the prosecution that had to bring that fact into evidence.

"And so, I must ask again, where are these people who will show these 'drastic' changes in Mr. Lee? I contend that there has been no showing of any 'drastic' change in the personality of this defendant. I contend that it is not sufficient to say that his hairstyle changed, that he decided to drop out of school, that he wanted to try anal sex, that he didn't bathe as often as he should. These things are insufficient and lacking in relevance to the matter of appropriate punishment for this dastardly crime."

From the final summary for the defense of Daniel Lee:

"The District Attorney points out that the fact that Daniel's hair grew long is not very important; and, in and of itself, I suppose it isn't. However, when it is considered along with the fact that he stopped bathing, that he ceased caring about the cleanliness of his room and his car, that he developed an aversion for insects that did not exist previously, that his sexual interests turned bizarre and seemed all consuming, all of that taken together paints a vivid picture of an individual who has problems—more severe problems than anyone imagined at the time.

"Now obviously, our evidence did not impress the District Attorney. He made light of it. He posed the question, 'Where are these witnesses who will testify to the drastic changes that took place in the defendant?'

"Well, God almighty! Where was he when they were testifying? I thought he was sitting right there! Could he not hear? Would he not hear? He said some of the changes were insignificant. Well, some of them were. It was a very gradual

process that was taking place. It was an insidious process, a sort of creeping paralysis of the conscience. However, when the totality of the changes—when what he was is compared with what he became—then the changes are not only significant, they are shocking! Can anyone say that a significant change has not taken place when an individual, who has seemingly enjoyed a normal sex life, suddenly purchases a blow-up doll to make love to for Christ's sake?

"And if the State sincerely believed that a dramatic change did not come over this boy, why didn't they get someone to come forward and testify to that fact? Why didn't they get someone to say, he's always been bad news or he kicked my dog or he stole my bicycle? Surely someone would have been willing to strike a lick at this boy!

"Surely, surely, if Daniel Lee was not a loving and kind individual before the aneurysm, the State could have found someone who would have testified as much. And just as surely, if this boy did not change into a slovenly, uncaring, self-centered, sexually demented wretch after the aneurysm, they could have found someone to testify to that, too. Couldn't they? Well, couldn't they? Maybe not."

CHAPTER FIFTEEN
THE DOCTOR

Dr. James Lindley was not the surgeon who operated on Daniel Lee at Baptist Hospital. He was, however, the Chief Resident in Neurosurgery at the hospital, and he was involved in the follow-up examinations of the defendant. At the request of the defense team, he engaged in a thorough study of the medical records pertaining to the case. Lindley was accustomed to testifying as an expert witness in court cases. He was certified by the court and accepted as an expert witness.

From the witness stand and at Mr. Whittle's request, the doctor described the defendant's diagnosis and injury: "The incident was a subarachnoid hemorrhage related to an aneurysm rupture. The problem was very serious—even life threatening. About one third of patients who experience such bleeds never make it to the hospital. Of those who do make it to the hospital, many do not do well. Either they die from complications or are left severely impaired. Another third does very well. They return home and lead normal lives. However, they may be left with some sort of neurological deficit, which might evidence itself in the form of difficulty with speech, slow thinking, or maybe weakness on one side of the body.

"A craniotomy was performed on Daniel Lee to place a clip on his aneurysm. The goal in such a procedure is to separate the aneurysm from the vessel from which it grew. The operation was necessary because aneurysms are prone to re-bleed. The clip can sometimes prevent that. Metal retractors were used to pull the frontal lobes of Mr. Lee's brain back. Deep within the brain the vessels are usually wrapped around each other. Important feeding vessels carry blood to vital areas. Even though these vessels are small, injury to them can have grave consequences."

Whittle inquired, "Do you know whether any damage was done in the surgery or whether Daniel lost any brain tissue during the surgery?"

"Absolutely, there was and he did. There is always a certain amount of brain damage incurred in retracting the brain. In this case, they actually had to dissect a small amount of brain, silent brain, to get to the aneurysm. It's been shown to be less costly to do that than to try to retract the whole frontal lobe."

"I understand you examined the defendant at Baptist Hospital after he was charged with these crimes. Is that true, and if it is, what did you find?"

Lindley perused his notes briefly and then responded, "Yes, on March 27, 1990, he underwent a neurological examination. We did a CAT scan of the head, with and without intravenous, contrast infusion. We discovered that he had suffered some infarction or stroke. Dark spaces were discovered on the scan, areas of dead or non-functioning brain. The spaces were in the region of the brain at the caudate nuclei. That particular area is thought to be associated with the motor system—walking, talking, things like that. The scan was objective evidence of damage to that portion of the brain."

"During your examination, did you elicit any new history?"

"Yes, he reported some problems: sweating episodes, headaches, and other minor things. We performed a neurostatus examination, which is a routine kind of thing. It has to do with his orientation and mood. Is he alert? Is he coherent? Is he quiet? Agitated? Belligerent? What's his memory like? His speech?"

"And what did you find?"

"Well, Mr. Whittle, I felt it was remarkable for the fact that he seemed either unconcerned or unaware—and in my opinion, it was unconcerned—at the alarming state of his circumstances. I referred to the charges against him and the pending trial. He was very willing to talk about it, but he seemed emotionally unaffected."

"And what significance did you assign to that, sir?"

"It was significant in my opinion. It's an abnormal finding."

"Are there areas in the region of Daniel's brain damage, Doctor Lindley, that have an effect on behavior?"

"Not classically or specifically. But we must think of pathways that go through the areas where the damage is located. These areas may have been damaged because of the damage to a small supply artery called the Recurrent Artery Huebner. It would not be uncommon to have damage to one of these arteries related to an aneurysm on one side or the other. But I have never heard of a patient who had infarcts on both sides. I was very surprised to see these infarcts. I have never seen them on both sides. And the fact that they are bilateral indicates more significance than unilateral. So, he's injured as a result of subarachnoid hemorrhage; and a little more has probably been injured as a result of the surgery. And then, when you add in the fact that some of his outflow tracks have also been cut off on both sides, then there is certainly the potential for some drastic behavior change."

"Is his condition permanent, doctor?

"His infarcts are very permanent."

"Is there a medicine or treatment that will help him."

"Not to my knowledge."

"Doctor, are neurosurgeons really concerned with the behavior of their patients after surgery?"

"Certainly, we are; however, our primary responsibility is, I think, the physical functioning. For instance: Can they move their eyes? Can they walk around and be independent? Those things are our primary concerns."

"Are there fields, doctor, which do deal with the behavior following surgery such as this?"

"Yes, sir. That's what neuropsychologists and neuropsychiatrists do."

"Thank you, doctor, that's all I have, your Honor."

Judge Lamm invited the prosecution to question the doctor. Mr. Wilson approached the witness stand: "Doctor, I will be brief, but I do have a few questions—mainly just clarifications. Did I understand you to say that the damaged area of the defendant's brain is believed to be a back-up to the motor system—moving of arms and legs, things of that nature?"

"Yes, Mr. Wilson. A typical injury in the basal ganglia causes things like Huntington's Chorea and Parkinsonism, severe movement disorders."

"You mentioned damage to the Artery of Huebner? And I think you said that relates to a weakness in one's limbs and such? What we laymen might describe as a stroke?"

"Yes sir."

"And you said the defendant was lethargic or ..."

"I would describe what we found as a 'flat' affect. He was awake. He was with it. He was just not affected emotionally."

"Could prolonged use of marijuana or alcohol or a combination of the two cause such symptoms?"

"I suppose it's possible, but I don't really know. I don't deal with that on a regular basis in any more than a superficial manner with the patients I see."

"Now, you said it was possible—your words—that some of the things you have observed could cause a personality change. You're not testifying that the injury did cause a personality change, but only that it is possible. Is that correct?

"That's correct. When I saw the CAT scan, I was very much struck by it; and I couldn't help but think that it's possible that such a change in behavior could occur. And then I remembered reading about some lesion experiments of the past. These experiments were done on animals. And it turns out that when these experiments were done on cats, bilateral caudate lesions caused sustained derangement in personality, particularly in the area of sexual activity. Cats with damage on just one side were not very much affected. However, when the lesions were on both sides, like those of the defendant, the cats had a sustained change in their behavior for up to a year or as long as they were evaluated."

"Well, what you're saying now is very hypothetical or theoretical, isn't it, doctor?"

"Not so theoretical. We've seen it happen in cats."

"In cats, yes, but still very hypothetical?"

Doctor Lindley shrugged.

From the final summary for the State of North Carolina:

"You heard the testimony, ladies and gentlemen of the jury, of Dr. Lindley. He told you that Daniel Lee had some brain damage. He said it was in the motor skills area, that it caused a loss of some of his motor skills—the ability to move his arms and legs and such, that's all. The doctor did not confirm that the aneurysm had caused any change in behavior."

From the final summary for the defense of Daniel Lee:

"I told you we would produce witnesses who would attest to the seriousness of the trauma that occurred to Daniel's brain. You heard those witnesses testify to the serious nature of his condition. You heard Dr. Lindley say that his condition was touch and go for a time; it was life threatening. Daniel could have died on that operating table in 1988. In my opinion, and in a very real sense, he did die. No one has really seen the kind and considerate person that was Daniel Lee since his trip to Baptist Hospital.

"We presented you with the testimony of the best medical experts we could find. The Chief Resident in Neurosurgery at Baptist Hospital, Dr. Lindley, testified that the boy had definite, discernible, detectable, verifiable brain damage. He told us that damage similar to that suffered by Daniel caused deviant and aggressive sexual behavior in animals.

"Still, the District Attorney continues to ask: 'Has he no conscience? Has he no pity? Has he no mercy?'

"No, Mr. Rusher, he has none of those things. The medical experts are telling us that he lost them all on the operating table at Baptist Hospital!"

CHAPTER SIXTEEN
THE PSYCHOLOGIST

"Psychologists study human emotions, behavior, learning, personality and intellect," was Dr. Anthony Sciara's response to Chester Whittle's inquiry related to the service provided by members of his profession. The doctor performed a very thorough and comprehensive psychological examination of Daniel Lee on behalf of the defense. He was imminently qualified to carry out such duties. So imminently qualified was he that the length and breadth of his credentials seemed interminable as he relayed them to the court: he was not only a member of almost every professional psychological association imaginable, he was—or had been—an officer of most. He was a "Diplomat" of Clinical Psychology, the highest level of practice in the field. His papers were routinely published both nationally and internationally. Sciara was one of only five individuals in the country qualified to conduct workshops related to the Rorschach Ink Blot Test.

The doctor testified his forensic evaluation of Daniel Lee included the following measures: interviews with people who knew the defendant both prior and subsequent to his aneurysm, psychological testing (including the Rorschach Ink Blot Test and the Weschler Adult Intelligence Scale Revised), and neuropsychological testing (including the Halsted Ratan Neuropsychological Test Battery). In addition, the doctor reviewed Daniel Lee's medical records from the Watauga County Medical Center, the North Carolina Baptist Hospital, and the Dorothea Dix Hospital. He perused books from his own library and those of others and consulted with colleagues in Alabama, North Carolina, and Virginia, related to appropriate or associated neurobehavioral disorders.

Mr. Whittle's first question to Dr. Sciara went right to the heart of the trial: "Doctor, do you have an opinion as to whether Daniel Brian Lee's capacity to appreciate the criminality of his conduct or to conform his conduct to the requirements of the law was impaired?"

"Yes, I do and it was. It's my opinion that he could appreciate his conduct. He did know what he was doing was wrong —that those behaviors were not appropriate. He did know that. But could he control his behavior? No, he had a problem there. It was that behavioral control that went out on him and led to his committing these terrible crimes."

"And how did you arrive at that opinion, sir?"

"Neuropsychology, Mr. Whittle, is a field where we have developed a number of what we call non-invasive tests. These are tests where we're not sticking things into anybody; we're not cutting them open. We're having them perform tasks for observation. It's through the observation of the performance of the tasks that we gain information about how well the brain of the subject is functioning. Do they do things on these tests the way normal people do them? Are they in the normal range? The results allow us to compare the person against normal people and to look for signs that are different from normal.

"The battery of tests we gave the defendant took essentially all of one day to administer. The results of the tests were surprising. They seemed to indicate that the patient was not significantly impaired.

"Oh, there were some signs. His memory for items presented visually was not equal to his memory for things presented verbally. They should be equal. His sensation in his right hand was diminished. We discovered that his strength of grip on both hands was quite a bit lower than what would be expected for a male of his size and age. But, again, the findings were not as significant as I expected.

"I was surprised because I knew that the CAT scans

showed that there was brain damage. Given the reality that he had his skull opened, that they were moving the brain around, that they worked in there—clipping things off and such—people generally show some deficits or problems. I expected to find signs of brain damage, but the tests reflected only a small amount of damage. So that part of my exam bothered me, and that's why I wanted to interview people to see if he was different from before the aneurysm until after the aneurysm."

"And did you conduct those interviews, Dr. Sciara? And is that an accepted part of psychological testing?"

"Yes sir, it is. And I did do the interviews. It is the best way, and the recommended way, to tap into problems with the frontal lobe of the brain. I interviewed seven people. In summary, they indicated to me that there were many personality changes in Mr. Lee. His personal hygiene and general cleanliness got significantly worse than it had been. He essentially lost his ambition to succeed or to work. His drive to set goals and to plan ahead to fulfill those goals was no longer present. His willingness to think of people in a considerate manner changed.

"So, the individuals interviewed were giving me a rather consistent picture of changes in the defendant's behavior and affect. When we talk about affect, we're talking about emotion. We all feel things that happen to us or that happen in the world. When we watch a sad movie, we might begin to cry. It's a normal response. When we don't respond normally, then that's a change or what we refer to as a 'flatness' of affect. What I found with Daniel Lee was that he offered a rather consistent flat affect—he, basically, just had no emotion."

"And what, sir, is your opinion of his psychological condition if ..."

"Well," Sciara anticipated the question, "he's a pretty classically brain-damaged individual. And that is a permanent condition; plus, frequently 'bleeds' such as the one experienced by the defendant, will reoccur. It's hard to predict the future in relation to his condition. I'm confident he will not get particularly better; he might not get worse. We will continue to see a lack of control of behavior. We'll see an inability to stop behaviors once they get started and an inability to initiate lots of planned or goal directed behavior.

"Mr. Lee suffered a subarachnoid hemorrhage. Almost no one escapes such a problem without some psychosocial problem. Even if the problem is minor, patients, whenever they suffer a bleed, do have problems related to that bleed. When the problems in this area produce bilateral, medial, frontal-lobe infarction, as is the case here, dramatic consequences may result."

"Doctor, if he had been told he was changing or had changed, could he have modified his behavior?"

"I don't think so. Many such patients get so out of control that their families must take some action to put them in a secure environment. Often the only answer is to put the person in a secure, structured environment. In this case, a structured environment such as a prison would work for Daniel, a place where he's told what to do and when to do it. I found consistently in the psychological testing that he would do what he was told to do."

Whittle thanked the doctor and declared an end to the questioning for the defense. Mr. Rusher arose quickly and began his interrogation enthusiastically, "You're not a psychiatrist; you're a psychologist. Is that right doctor?"

"That's correct, sir."

"You do not take people's temperature, nor do you prescribe medication."

"Correct again."

"When people come to you for services, they are clients rather than patients?"

"No, they are patients, or they are clients. The terms are used interchangeably."

"You have indicated, doctor, that you have testified in other cases as an expert witness. Approximately how many times have you testified in criminal cases?"

"I don't have a count for you, Mr. Rusher; however, I would say the number of times is significant."

"You have never testified for the State, have you? And in every capital case where you have testified, you have expressed your opinion, have you not, that the capital felony was committed while the defendant was under the influence of mental or emotional disturbance, is that not true?"

"I have worked for the State on cases, but I think I have not testified on behalf of the State. And I don't think it is accurate to say that every time I have testified I reported the defendant suffered from a mental disturbance."

"In every case I can find you have expressed your opinion that the capacity of the defendant to appreciate the criminality of his conduct or to conform his conduct to the requirements of the law was impaired. Have I missed something?"

"Well, truly, Mr. Rusher, I do not recall. Each case is different, and each case would have different psychological factors bearing on it. When, if I may explain, when you ask me about those things, what you're asking about are legal terms. The question does not relate to psychological terms. What happens in those cases is that the psychological description of the person is then forced into a legal classification so that it can be understood in terms of the law. So, what you are trying to do is to take a bunch of apples and make orange juice out of them. It's hard because you're talking about different concepts."

"What I'm trying to say, doctor, is this: you always wind up finding something useful that you can say for any defendant in any criminal case. Now, isn't that right?"

"No, it is not right at all. What I try to do is honestly describe that person and their psychological, intellectual, and neuropsychological functioning. The reality of the matter is that people who get into trouble with the law often have impairments in those areas. This is not strange, nor is it unrealistic. We often find that people who get into trouble with the law frequently have mental or emotional impairments. Actually, that's only logical. That does not mean I'm an advocate for that person. I'm not. All I'm doing is describing what I see."

"And you receive quite a large fee for doing that, don't you, sir?"

"I'm paid for my services by the State."

"And you realize that you have become a particularly hot item in terms of your ability to say things for defendants in criminal cases? You know that, don't you?"

Mr. Whittle objected to the question. Judge Lamm sustained the objection and directed the District Attorney to "move along." Rusher brushed off the rebuff and advanced on a new front. "You have indicated, doctor, that you are an expert on the Rorschach Ink Blot Test. Is that test something you viewed as significant toward interpreting Daniel Lee's behavior?"

"Yes. The test is helpful in determining how people perceive things, how people cope, whether or not they have disordered thinking. It provides a lot of information."

"Do you have your ink blots with you, sir?"

"Well, yes, in a miniature fashion and without color. You see, some of the blots have color and the fact that they do is important."

"Doctor, let me draw your attention to the third blot on the top row. Now, what does that portray?"

Smiling, the doctor responded, "It's an ink blot, Mr. Rusher."

"It's an ink blot? So, you're saying it could be anything at all?"

"No, sir. It couldn't be anything at all. It couldn't be the Empire State Building. It couldn't be this courtroom. There are a lot of things it could not be. However, if someone were to respond that it is the Empire State Building, we would then score that as what we call a minus response. It would be an inappropriate response for that blot."

"Now as to this particular blot, you often get the response that it represents two men in combat, is that not true? With blood all around? Do you not frequently get that response?"

Sciara looked at the blot incredulously and then peered back into the face of the District Attorney, "Mr. Rusher, I've been administering this test for years, and I believe you are the first person who has ever seen that blot in that way. I learn something new every day."

Chuckles emanated from the gallery and the jury box. Even Judge Lamm was forced to stifle a smile. Rusher scarcely noticed, and continued to bore in, "Well, do you get the response that it portrays two men?"

"Sometimes."

"And if you got a response that it portrayed two women, would that be unusual?"

"Maybe, maybe not. We typically don't take responses out of context, Mr. Rusher. So, if on one card someone says it's a bat and on the same card someone else says it's a butterfly, it really doesn't make much difference. What we do is code each response through a sophisticated coding system. When we are finished assigning the category codes to the response, we then summarize that and put it together in certain formulas that relate to real world behaviors. Anytime a response is pulled out of context, it has no meaning. We can talk about two men in bloody combat; however, it has no meaning unless we can summarize all of the scores from the test."

"I understand that it was from showing the defendant these ten cards with ink blots on them that you drew your conclusions about this case?"

"Well, no. The Rorschach is but one tool of the process. Interviews are another important facet of the process."

"Did you interview Daniel Lee?"

"I did."

"Did you ask him what his perception was as he was striking Jeni Gray over the head with a club?"

"I don't know that I asked that specific question. I asked

him how he killed Ms. Gray. He said he hit her with a stick and then strangled her."

"Since you have the ability to express an opinion as to what his perception was, tell us about his feelings as he was beating Jeni Gray."

"I'm glad you asked that question, Mr. Rusher. It's an important one. And the answer is that his feelings were quite different from normal. He may indeed have been feeling nothing. Did he know what he was doing? I think so. But there was no *feeling* attached to the knowing. You see, it's that 'flat' affect we've been talking about."

"In the report you have given me, you have indicated that there are really no reliable tests to give to make a diagnosis or to draw opinions from such a case as Daniel Lee's, is that correct?"

"Yes, the way we evaluate is through clinical interviews with people who knew the patient before and after the onset of the problem."

"Well, if you have no reliable tests, then the tests you gave were essentially useless, is that correct?"

"No. You're misstating that the tests are not reliable. They are. They indicate brain damage. The other evaluation procedure is the interviews. That is what is taught."

"You have indicated, doctor, that the defendant knew at all times he was acting wrong, haven't you?"

"Mr. Rusher, if you had said that he knew what he did was wrong, I would say yes. Did he know it at all times? I'm not certain. I think so. That's the best I can do."

"Well, in truth, you're not certain of anything you're saying, are you? You're speaking your opinion about things going on in somebody else's mind, are you not?"

"I'm speaking from the standpoint of a professional evaluation,"

"Right."

"Just as I should be, Mr. Rusher."

"When the defendant told Leigh Cooper of the things he

had done to Jeni Gray, he gave an emotional response. He was boasting, wasn't he?"

"You'll have to define for me what you mean by 'boasting,' because I'm not sure I understand you."

"You don't understand the word 'boast?'"

"I'm not sure I understand it in the way you're using it."

"Do you at all recognize, sir, that some people do things just because they are evil people!"

"Yes."

"You have given testimony about a single event that took place in the defendant's life—the aneurysm—as being of primary importance in what he is now. But other things have happened throughout his life that have related to his character building, have they not?"

"Yes sir. No doubt about that. If I had to rank them, I would put the aneurysm at the top of the list; but, certainly, other factors apply."

Rusher paused at the prosecution table for an extended interval to examine his notes. Finally, he looked up and fired a parting shot at the doctor: "If he was totally devoid of emotion, Dr. Sciara, he would not have boasted to Leigh Cooper what he did to Jeni Gray, would he?"

"You'll have to define 'boasted' for me before I can do that, Mr. Rusher."

"Well, no, that's okay. Your Honor, that's all I have of him."

From the final summary for the State of North Carolina:

"I would like, at this time, to address the testimony of Dr. Sciara for you ladies and gentlemen of the jury. You certainly remember Dr. Sciara; he was an important witness for the defense, a very important witness for the defense. In fact, it is largely upon his testimony that the defense rests.

"What do we know about Dr. Sciara? We know he is not a medical doctor; he is a psychologist. We don't know if he has some practice in psychology or not. He didn't tell us. He said he had articles published nationally and internationally, but he never told us the titles of them or in what books or maga-

zines or periodicals they could be found. He told us all of these great things about himself; and then he said, in essence, that he knows for a fact that brain damage caused the defendant to commit these terrible crimes.

"Well, let's think about this for a minute. Here is a man who has talked with the defendant twice in his life. He has run some simple tests, which by his own admission returned essentially normal results. He talked to seven people, mainly family members and friends of the accused; and now he has arrived at the inescapable conclusion that Daniel Lee could not control his actions.

"Dr. Sciara performed a number of tests on the defendant. Most of the results, he admits, were normal. One test performed by the doctor indicated that the defendant had below average strength in his hands. Well, we all know—and all too well!—that the defendant possessed sufficient strength to grip a club and bring it down on the head of Jeni Gray with enough force to crush her skull. Apparently Mr. Daniel Lee did not demonstrate all of his strength for Dr. Sciara.

"In interviews with the defendant, the doctor found what he called a 'flat' affect' an absence of emotion. Well, he only interviewed him twice. Both times he was in jail. What did he expect? Truth is, Mr. Lee doesn't have a whole lot to get excited about right now. He's at a sort of low ebb. As a result of this trial, he's either going to die or be in prison the rest of his life. I would like to point out, however, that he got pretty excited when he had Leigh Cooper as a captive in his car. He was pretty dog-gone hyper when he was forcing her suffering and boasting about that suffering he had inflicted upon Jeni Gray.

"Dr. Sciara puts a lot of stock in ink blots. He says he can tell if a person is crazy or not by studying an individual's reaction to ink that has blotted on a page. If you believe he can, then you should weigh his testimony accordingly.

"When not engaged in the study of spilled ink, the doctor was conducting interviews. Did it seem to you, as it did to me, that he chose to interview people who might be expected to say things that would work to the advantage of the defendant? He interviewed Mr. Lee's father. He interviewed his sister. He interviewed his girlfriend.

"Allow me, ladies and gentlemen, to remind you of something else about this psychologist before you place great stock in his testimony. Although he is a highly educated man, he didn't know the meaning of the word 'boast.' Now 'boast' is not a hard word. It's not a fancy word. It's a common, everyday word. It's an emotional word. Why, I knew that when Daniel Lee told Leigh Cooper that he had killed Jeni Gray, that he had hit her over the head with a club, that he had kicked her in the throat, that he had strangled the life out of her, he was boasting! If I knew that, a highly educated man like a psychologist ought to know that!

"Dr. Sciara did say one thing that I think was significant, very significant. You will recall that I asked him if the aneurysm was the sole cause of the defendant's problems or if other factors such as a lifetime of learning and experience were interrelated with his problems. The doctor's answer was that all of those things are interrelated.

"So, in the end, all of these things cannot be understood by ink that has blotted on a page, nor interviews with family and friends. If he had no conscience, then at least part of his condition preceded the aneurysm or was never completely developed."

From the final summary for the defense of Daniel Lee:

"The prosecution attempts to dismantle the testimony of Dr. Sciara by implying that he is some sort of 'on call' witness for the defense. Now, if this line of thinking is carried to its logical conclusion, there must be a catalog of 'experts for the prosecution.' Why didn't the District Attorney simply look up the closest prosecution expert and have that person refute the testimony of Dr. Sciara?

"Well, the truth of the matter is that there are no such catalogs of biased experts; but the question remains: Why didn't the State have expert testimony refuting that of Dr.

Sciara? I mean surely the State of North Carolina could find some doctor who would come forward and attempt to discredit our witnesses' findings. One must wonder: Why didn't they?

"Dr. Sciara did a thorough and a professional job. He explained his methods. He applied the appropriate non-invasive diagnostic tests; he collected information from interviews with individuals who knew Daniel before and after his surgery; he gave you his opinion relating to why Daniel behaved in such an abhorrent manner. He said his brain was damaged in such a way that he could not control nor appreciate his actions.

"The State wants to know why Dr. Sciara interviewed only people who were close to the defendant. Well, you members of the jury are not psychologists; but just tell me, who would you interview if you wanted to compare an individual's behavior before a certain event with their behavior after the event? It would have to be someone who knew the person before the event and after the event, wouldn't it? You wouldn't go out and ask some poor soul strolling down the street, would you? Common sense dictated who was interviewed.

"Mr. Rusher clearly does not put much stock in the Rorschach Ink Blot Test. It seems not to matter that the test is widely accepted in professional, psychological circles as being a valid and useful tool in understanding human behavior. The District Attorney seems to feel that his own superficial knowledge is of greater importance than that of an entire field of scientific inquiry. He apparently feels his own judgment should carry more weight than the experience of a man with impeccable, professional credentials who has made his life's work the understanding of maladies of the human mind.

"The prosecution makes much of the statement that the defendant's problems cannot be attributed to his aneurysm alone. The State shines a bright light on the statement by Dr.

Sciara that other factors may have contributed to the degree of abnormal behavior exhibited by the defendant. However, it should be pointed out that the Doctor's report found, and the fact remains, that if the aneurysm had not occurred, the crimes would not have been committed. I believe the defense accomplished what it set out to do. In every instance we provided testimony and/or evidence to support the claims that were made."

CHAPTER SEVENTEEN
The State's Summary

At the conclusion of Mr. Rusher's cross examination of Dr. Sciara, Judge Lamb recessed the court for the day. He asked the District Attorney to be prepared to make his final arguments when court reconvened at 10 a.m. the following morning.

(The final summaries for the two lawyers for the prosecution and the two for the defense were lengthy and detailed; sixty-nine pages were transcribed by the court recorder. A significant portion of the final summaries has been shared at what were deemed the appropriate and proximate times for their inclusion in this book. The "sum-up" or the closing comments from the final summaries follow now.)

Wednesday, April 25, 1990. District Attorney Tom Rusher for the State of North Carolina:

"May it please the Court, counsel at the bar, ladies and gentlemen of the jury. It seems like quite a long time ago when I stood before you and made an opening statement; but, in fact, it was only last week when I forecasted for you what the State's evidence would show. At that time, you knew nothing about this case. Now you know the defendant has admitted his guilt, and you are charged to determine the appropriate punishment for his crimes. The facts are in; the evidence has been presented. You are now aware of everything you need to know in order to make an informed and proper decision regarding what the defendant's punishment should be.

"There's really not much more to say, more than has already been said. I think we all know the truth of the matter here. There has been no mitigation shown for these terrible

crimes. There has been no personality change shown which would mitigate by some mental disease this terrible crime. The defense here is void, the mitigation nonexistent.

"So, in closing, I wish to say that you have heard a lot of evidence in this case. You have heard the testimony of many witnesses. But there is one witness whose testimony you did not hear. If she could have testified, we wouldn't be engaged in this trial. I speak, of course, of Jeni Gray. Mr. Daniel Lee prevented her appearance. He led her down the Jake's Mountain Road and into the valley of the shadow of death. Then he came out alone. He left her there. Mr. Daniel Lee did that, the man who had no mercy, the man who now begs mercy of you.

"Why capital punishment, ladies and gentlemen? It is because of the unusually cruel and inhumane manner in which Jeni's life was ended that we must take such drastic action. It is because of the fiendish methods of the murderer, the extraordinary cruelty displayed. Such an uncommon crime begs uncommon punishment. Life imprisonment is not appropriate, for it is just not adequate. It is insufficient. There is but one punishment appropriate for this man: he deserves no less than to die for his crimes!

"Your path is clear. It is the time to be strong. The State is obliged to ask you to cast out from the living this Daniel Brian Lee, for it was he who dared to pluck the very flower of humanity.

"These are the contentions of the State of North Carolina in this matter. Thank you for your service ladies and gentlemen of the jury, and may God send you."

Mr. Rusher seated himself as a hush descended upon the Court.

CHAPTER EIGHTEEN
Summary for the Defense

Judge Lamm intruded on the silence at the close of the summation for the prosecution to invite Mr. Whittle to summarize for the defense.

"Thank you, your Honor. May it please the Court, ladies and gentlemen of the jury, I will be the last lawyer to speak to you. And it is a heavy yoke of responsibility that I bear. My father is a lawyer, but nothing in my life has prepared me for this. Not going to Vietnam. Really, just not anything. I don't suppose anything has prepared you for this either.

"And I know Daniel Lee did terrible things. For me to say or imply anything less would be to deny my own humanity. I have been, just as you must be, torn by many emotions. Mostly, I think I have just been overwhelmed. In spite of my years of experience, I have felt—and still feel—inadequate to the task of defending this man.

"This trial started out as a rather civilized and orderly affair. We were all calm, collected, and professional. When you were selected as jurors, the District Attorney asked if you could decide this case without prejudice and without passion; however, he just completed an eloquent and emotional and passionate plea for you to kill this boy. At first, he wanted jurors; now, he wants executioners.

"I mean, really, did you feel you were being asked to make a rational decision during the summary for the prosecution? Or did you feel, as I did, that a bitter demand for revenge was issuing forth? Did you perceive any trace of understanding or compassion, or did you feel that, in order to achieve the end of another death, hatred was being spewed forth.

"The summary for the prosecution seemed directed at stirring a negative passion within you. It sought to arouse hate and anger. You might wish to ask yourself now: Am I angry? It's a good question. You know people make mistakes when they're angry. You agreed in the jury selection process to base your verdict on the truth—that's what 'verdict' means. You cannot base your decision on emotion. You promised not to.

"I would like to ask you, ladies and gentlemen of the jury, to examine and compare the methods employed by the defense and the prosecution in this case. Let's look at the outline for the defense first. To begin with, we admitted guilt. We acknowledged the heinous nature of the crimes and agreed that such crimes should never be allowed to be repeated.

"We did not ask for freedom; we set out to show that certain factors existed in this affair that make the defendant's behavior—not forgivable—but maybe, just maybe, in the context of a damaged brain, at least fathomable. We demonstrated through evidence that Daniel's behavior changed. We showed you what kind of person he was before the aneurysm, and we showed you what kind of person he became. The expert with the greatest expertise in the most closely associated field told you that it was his opinion that the damage suffered by Daniel's brain led to the commission of these terrible crimes.

"Now, let's look at the case for the prosecution for a moment. The State set out to prove that the crime was a terrible one, that it was deplorable. The State did a fine job. But please, give me a break. That wasn't hard to prove, was it? For the crime WAS terrible; it WAS deplorable. But didn't we know that from the outset? However, I must admit, the State did a good job of demonstrating and, lest we forget, constantly reminding us of the blows that were struck and the things that were said. But beyond demonstrating the heinous nature of the crime, what else did the prosecution

prove? Where is the rest of their case?

"By repeatedly emphasizing the lurid aspects of the crime, it seems that the State is contending that this boy is just evil—not brain damaged but evil. Well, if he wasn't brain damaged and he wasn't stupid, how does the State explain some of the bizarre actions of the defendant? For instance, he has a real gun at home, but he chooses a B.B. gun to carry during his criminal endeavors. He murders a lovely young girl in a savage manner, but then makes no effort to conceal her body. He decides to take his next victim home, but when she says she wants something to eat, he leaves her alone in the car and goes to get her a snack. His victim escapes and he saunters on home as if nothing happened. And then, of course, just as sure as God made little, green apples, the police come along and take him in. If brain damage is not the explanation for these occurrences, then what is?

"You will recall that the State said it was time for you to be strong, to have courage. Well, the defense agrees. It is indeed the time for you to be strong. But sometimes it takes more strength to love than it does to hate. You must know by now that your friends and your associates are counting on you to kill Daniel Lee. They have certainly read of the terrible things he has done; they will expect you to repay him in like kind. They will not understand if you sentence him to life imprisonment; for they, don't you see, will only be aware of the sensational aspects of this case, the brutal, cruel aspects upon which the State has dwelled.

"They will be unaware of the detailed medical testimony. They will not know of the evidence you have seen pertaining to the changes that came over the defendant. They will not know of the great likelihood that a weakness in the wall of a minute blood vessel set in motion a sequence of events that led to unbelievable human tragedy. They cannot know that duty and fairness require you to look beyond the sensational, the sordid, the demented, to see the truth that the dispensing of justice is not simple and sometimes

requires an awesome measure of intelligence and maturity.

"I'm speaking about love here folks. Somewhere, some-how, all of this has got to end. Let's end it here. Violence begets violence. Force calls forth more force. Hate begets hate. To execute a person with brain damage is to demean this State and this nation. Has our great State come to that? Have we come to that?

"It has been said that the man who had no mercy now asks mercy of you. I would like to point out that it no longer matters what the defendant had and what he failed to give. The question is now upon you members of the jury. What is it that you have to give? What is inside you? Is it revenge and hatred or is it compassion and understanding? Can you look upon the pitiless shell the defendant has become and still find love within your own heart? Can you remember that Jesus don't hate sinners—he hates sin.

"So, it is I who ask for mercy for the defendant. And, re-ally, I ask it for all of us who share the responsibility in this process we call justice. We must be careful, for if we choose to kill this boy, we will not bring Jeni back, we will not right a wrong, we will not vanquish the beast that dwells within Daniel Lee. We may just replace it. We may just become the beast.

"These are the contentions of the defense in this case, members of the jury. We join our learned colleagues of the prosecution in wishing you Godspeed in your deliberations."

The silence at the conclusion of the summary for the de-fense was as palpable as it had been for the prosecution.

CHAPTER NINETEEN
The End

"Members of the jury," Judge Charles Lamm began, "the defendant, Daniel Brian Lee, has pled guilty to murder in the first degree. It is now your duty to recommend to the Court whether he should be sentenced to death or to life imprisonment. All of the evidence relevant to your recommendation has been presented. It is now your duty to decide, from all of the evidence presented, what the facts are and what his punishment should be. You will retire now to begin your deliberations."

A preliminary vote taken by the jury just to assess their position was nine to three in favor of the death penalty. Further consideration would be needed to achieve unanimity.

Four hours after the beginning of deliberations, Judge Lamm called for the jury to return to the courtroom. He addressed them, "I received your request for clarification. You have asked, and I quote, 'If he is sentenced to life, will he be eligible for parole at any time?'

"Let me instruct you as follows: the court imposes the punishment that the defendant will receive. The question of eligibility for parole is not a proper matter for you to consider in recommending punishment. It should be eliminated entirely from your consideration and dismissed from your minds.

"In considering whether to recommend death or life imprisonment, you should determine the question as though life imprisonment means exactly what the Statute says: 'imprisonment in the State's prison for life.' You should decide the question of punishment according to the issues submitted to you by the Court wholly uninfluenced by consideration of what another arm of the government might or might not do in the future. Please now return and resume your deliberations."

Clearly, at least three of the jurors agreed with Mr. Whittle's assessment that, "Somewhere, somehow, all of this has got to end. Violence begets violence. Force begets force. Hate begets hate." However, the ultimate truth, given the Judge's ruling regarding life imprisonment, was that there was only one way to be absolutely certain Daniel Lee would never kill again—only one.

At 4:40 p.m. on April 26,1990, the bailiff entered the courtroom and announced, "The jury has reached its verdict." A flurry of activity resulted. The courtroom was quickly filled to capacity. Individuals pushed and shoved to gain the last standing room available.

The Judge requested, "Madame Foreman, please stand. Have you reached a verdict?"

"Yes sir, we have. It is our unanimous recommendation that the defendant be sentenced to death."

"Is that the verdict, so say all of you?"

As the members of the jury replied in the affirmative, media representatives rushed to the exits to announce the verdict to their respective agencies. Lamm looked to the defense table and asked the defendant to stand. "Do you have anything to say before this court passes sentence upon you, Mr. Lee?"

"No, sir."

"Well, then, having pled guilty to murder in the first degree and the jury assembled at this term of Superior Court of Avery County having unanimously recommended a punishment of death, it is therefore adjudged and decreed that you be sentenced to death. Sheriff Lyons shall, forthwith, deliver said prisoner, Daniel Brian Lee, to the Warden of the State's Penitentiary in Raleigh, North Carolina, who shall cause said prisoner to be put to death as by law provided. May God have mercy on your soul, sir."

Daniel Lee was, per instructions, delivered to Central Prison in Raleigh, where he resided on death row for seven years during his appeals. His hair grew to his shoulders again. His teeth and the skin between his fingers turned brown from the cigarettes he chain-smoked. His appeals, one after the other, were denied; however, prior to his final appeal, he suffered one of the recurrent "bleeds" predicted by his doctors. He cheated his executioner and died of a cerebral hemorrhage on death row on January 11, 1997.

Not so long after the trial of Daniel Lee, Leigh Martin Cooper became Leigh Cooper Wallace when she married Christopher (Chris) Harold Wallace. Over the next several years the couple ushered two lovely children into the world: Jacob Christopher Wallace and Haleigh Lynn Wallace. Leigh became a widely recognized advocate, on a local and even a national basis, for rape victim's rights. She followed the advice of Mr. Rusher and devoted herself to the wide range of joyful potential that life offered her. She did so robustly and confidently until she was stricken with pneumonia and passed away on December 17, 2012.

On December 20, 2012, a memorial ceremony was held at the gymnasium of Watauga High School where Leigh was employed as a teacher, coach, and mentor for students. Thousands attended the service; all seats were filled; people stood outside in the rain to hear the tributes over the speaker system—and the tributes were many. Clearly, this story involved more than one "flower of humanity." The first, Jeni Gray, was designated by District Attorney Tom Rusher in his final summary for the State of North Carolina; the second was Leigh Cooper Wallace. May they both rest in peace.

Chris Wallace and Leigh Cooper Wallace, 1989

Leigh Cooper Wallace, 2010

Author's Note

This is, I think the reader will admit, a sad story. Actually, an exceedingly sad story. In an effort to achieve some measure of positive result, the author has agreed to donate proceeds from the book to scholarships in the names of Jeni Gray and Leigh Cooper Wallace. Those wishing to expand the positive result from a sad story are encouraged to pass this book to another along with the suggestion that the price they might have paid could be directed to help the young people who benefit from the scholarships.

Checks should be directed as follows: Payable to: ASU Foundation, Inc. Jeni Gray Scholarship Fund and sent to Appalachian State University, Boone, N.C. 28608 or Payable to the Leigh Cooper Wallace Scholarship Fund at Watauga High School, Boone, North Carolina 28607

—Wayne Clawson, April 2018

Made in the USA
Columbia, SC
11 May 2018